MAN
OF THE
CENTURY

Also by Richard Harrity and Ralph G. Martin
ELEANOR ROOSEVELT: HER LIFE IN PICTURES
THE HUMAN SIDE OF F.D.R.
MAN OF DESTINY: DE GAULLE OF FRANCE

MAN
OF THE
CENTURY
CHURCHILL

RICHARD HARRITY
AND
RALPH G. MARTIN

DUELL, SLOAN AND PEARCE, NEW YORK

CREDITS

Acme Newspictures, 88, 172

Aerofilm, 43 (bottom), 241

Barratt, 71 (top), 73

Bassano, 48 (top)

Bettman Archives, 27, 28 (bottom), 29 (top), 34 (right), 41 (top), 53 (top), 54 (right), 55 (bottom), 60 (bottom), 61 (bottom), 62 (both), 63 (top), 64 (top), 76, 77 (bottom), 89, 100 (both), 153 (top)

Birnback Publishing Service, 59 (top), 117 (top), 130 (top), 215 (bottom)

British Information Service, 2 (top), 3 (bottom), 4 (bottom), 13 (bottom), 58 (bottom), 77 (middle), 108, 144 (top), 151 (bottom), 154, 155 (top), 155 (bottom, right), 158 (both), 182, 186, 188, 195, 202 (bottom), 208 (bottom), 210 (top), 211 (top), 216 (bottom), 226

British Official War Office, 190, 191, 208 (top)

Brown Brothers, 61 (top), 65 (top), 69 (top), 71 (bottom), 247

Central Press, 7 (bottom), 44 (top), 45 (top)

Nancy Cook, 193 (bottom)

Culver, 34 (bottom, left), 40, 42 (bottom), 43 (top), 52, 66 (top), 69 (bottom), 77 (top), 78 (top), 79 (top), 85 (top), 90 (both), 92 (top), 93, 94, 99 (both), 101 (bottom), 105, 109, 110 (top), 114, 146 (bottom), 155 (bottom, left)

Daily Herald, 37, 59 (bottom), 140, 181

Fox Photos, 10 (top), 125, 164, 235

Franklin D. Roosevelt Library, 9 (bottom), 66 (bottom), 184, 194 (top), 196, 199 (both), 212 (right), 213 (both), 222 (bottom)

Free-Lance Photographers Guild, Inc., 31, 50 (top), 95 (bottom), 97, 111, 117 (bottom), 118 (both), 119, 121, 124 (both), 126 (top), 128 (top), 138 (bottom), 149 (top), 170, 200 (top), 216 (top), 217, 223 (top), 232, 234 (top)

John R. Freeman, 45 (bottom)

French Embassy, Information and Press Division, 153 (bottom), 210 (bottom)

Gernsheim, 91

Harris & Ewing, 211 (bottom)

Hills & Saunders, 13 (top), 49 (top)

Illustrated London News, 37 (both), 128 (bottom)

Imperial War Museum, 47 (top), 113 (top), 174, 185, 201 (bottom), 206 (top), 207 (top)

Kemsley Picture Service, 5 (top), 6 (bottom), 8 (top), 11 (top), 98 (top), 129 (top), 147 (bottom), 202 (top), 223 (bottom), 225 (top)

Keystone, 151 (top), 209, 220 (bottom), 233 (bottom), 234 (bottom)

London Mirror Picture, 75, 81

London News Agency, 136 (bottom)

London Times, 44 (bottom)

Museum of the American Indian, 30 (both)

My African Journey, by Sir Winston Churchill, Hodder and Stoughton, 67 (both), 68 (both)

National Archives, 7 (top), 8 (bottom), 10 (top), 11 (bottom), 78 (bottom), 127 (top), 152 (bottom), 201 (top), 207 (bottom), 212 (left), 221, 225 (bottom), 238, 243

New York Daily News, 50 (bottom), 57 (top), 60 (top), 63 (bottom), 87, 130 (bottom), 131, 230

New York Genealogical Society, 23, 194 (bottom)

New York Public Library, 29 (middle, bottom), 32, 33, 34 (top), 35 (top), 41 (middle), 55 (top), 56, 58, 65 (bottom), 92 (bottom), 98 (bottom), 101 (top), 115, 244

Photographic News Agencies, 240

Picture Post, 163

Planet News, 138 (top), 242

Woodward Preston, 145

Radio Times Hulton Picture Library, 3 (top), 4 (top), 5 (bottom), 6 (top), 9 (top), 12 (bottom), 38, 39 (both), 46 (top), 47 (bottom), 48 bottom), 51, 53 (bottom), 54 (left), 57 (bottom), 70 (bottom), 74, 80, 83, 84 (both), 86 (bottom), 87, 95 (top), 96, 102, 103, 104, 106, 107, 112 (both), 116, 127 (bottom), 132 (bottom), 133, 134 (both), 167 (both), 168 (both), 169 (both), 173, 180, 200 (bottom), 222 (top), 233 (top)

The Remarkable Mr. Jerome, by Anita Leslie, Henry Holt & Co., Inc., and Hutchinson & Co., Ltd., 28 (top)

P. A. Reuter, 64 (bottom), 70 (top), 79 (bottom), 82

Edwin Rusczek, 26 (all)

Sons of the Revolution, 22

United Press International, 2 (bottom), 12 (top), 36, 113 (bottom), 129 (bottom), 132 (top), 136 (top), 162, 179, 219 (both), 227 (top), 228, 245, 246

United States Army Photograph, 189

Vivienne, 220 (top)

Wide World, 22, 110 (bottom), 120, 126 (bottom), 137, 139, 142, 143, 144 (bottom), 146 (top), 147 (top), 148 (left), 161, 165, 171, 176, 177, 183, 187, 193 (top), 197, 198, 206 (bottom), 214, 218 (both), 227 (bottom), 229 (both), 231, 237, 239

Our thanks are due for permission to quote from the following:

Second World War, by Sir Winston Churchill, published by Houghton Mifflin Company and Cassell & Co., Ltd.

Painting as a Pastime, by Sir Winston Churchill, published by McGraw-Hill Book Co., Inc., and Odhams Press Limited.

Savrola, by Sir Winston Churchill (Random House, 1956), reprinted by permission of Odhams Press Limited.

The material quoted on pages 17 and 20 and in the captions for the pictures on pages 46, 47, 48, 49, 50, 52, 53, 55, 57, 58, 59, 60, and 65 is reprinted with the permission of Charles Scribner's Sons from A Roving Commission (now published in the Scribner Library as My Early Life), pages 1, 3, 15, 17, 19, 27, 31, 40, 45, 60, 65, 124, 171, 183, 191, 206, 259, 270, 297, 318, by Winston Churchill. Copyright 1930 Charles Scribner's Sons, renewal copyright © 1958 Winston Churchill.

FIRST EDITION

Library of Congress Catalogue Card Number: 62-8521

Manufactured in the United States of America for Meredith Press

Duell, Sloan & Pearce

Affiliate of
MEREDITH PRESS
Des Moines & New York

For Lee Israel, a fine American photographer and a finer friend, who was wounded on D day, helping preserve those precious things Sir Winston prized, and who lived in London after the war and now lies buried in the England he, too, loved and served.

ACKNOWLEDGMENTS

In searching through some hundreds of thousands of pictures of Winston Churchill, everywhere from Stockbridge, Massachusetts, to South Africa—even to the point of searching an Indian cemetery with a flashlight at midnight to find a Churchill American ancestor—we have had the help of scores of people in many countries. We have taken care to give credit to every possible source. To those whom we have inadvertently overlooked, we apologize.

ENGLAND

To Doris R. Bryan our fullest appreciation for her important help.

Our warm thanks, too, to: Howard Byrne and Lee Israel, of Transatlantic News Features in London; A. J. Charge, Keeper of Pictures, and his staff at the Central Office of Information; John Hillelson, of Magnum Pictures; Evelyn Sheppard and Daphne Moss, of the Radio Times Hulton Picture Library; Archie Illingworth, Chief Guide of Blenheim Palace.

Our special thanks to Mr. Anthony Montague Browne, private secretary to Sir Winston Churchill.

To Gordon Robinson, Features Editor of the *Sunday Express,* our personal appreciation for his assistance.

FRANCE

Pierre Galante, of *Paris Match,* deserves our constant thanks for his help. We also express appreciation to Luva de Vysse, of Reporters Associés; Jean-Pierre Babelay; Kila Kugel; Mme. César Ritz; Michel St. Denis, Inspecteur Général du Théâtre Française; and Robert Garai, Agence Keystone Press in Paris.

SOUTH AFRICA

To Lieutenant Colonel Anthony Tebbitt, of Johannesburg, our thanks for his kindness and information.

UNITED STATES

Our indebtedness to: Sir Berkley Ormerod, Director of Public Relations of the British Information Services and his librarian, H. R. Isaacs, and the head of his Picture Division, Mrs. Nan McInally; Mrs. Graham Wilcox, Curator of the Stockbridge Library Association in Stockbridge, Massachusetts; Herman Kahn, Director of the Franklin D. Roosevelt Library in Hyde Park, and his most helpful staff; James Brewster and his staff at the Connecticut State Library; Mason Tolman, Reference Librarian of the New York State Library in Albany, and his assistants, Mary S. Lindsay and Ida M. Cohen; Mrs. Mildred Willcox Treen, Executive Secretary of the Sons of the Revolution of the State of New York; Jim Guadagno of the Museum of the American Indian; Miss Marie Berry, Executive Secretary of the New York Genealogical and Biographical Society; the staffs of the Museum of the City of New York, the New York State Historical Society, the Whitney Museum, the Yale University Library; and Mr. Jamie Kelly, County Historian in the Connecticut Hall of Records. Our added acknowledgment of appreciation to: G. Gelman, editor of the *Wallingford Post;* Gerald Harrington Miller, Town Clerk of Wallingford; and Mrs. Ernest Newell, a wonderful woman who has made her life a living history.

Special thanks to Mrs. Margaret H. Merhoff, head of the Wayne County Division of Archives and History in Lyons, New York, for her efforts in helping us check the Indian ancestry of Sir Winston Churchill.

More personally, our thanks to: Dan Mich, Editor of *Look* Magazine, who helped make this book possible; Beatrice and Bruce Gould and Mary Bass of the *Ladies Home Journal;* Edgar Peterson; Nelson Gruppo; Nancy Cook and Marion Dickerman; Dick Hanley; Jack Green; R. J. Birnback; D. Jay Culver and Marston Hamlin; Marty Monroe, Irma Masut, James Hernandez, Philip H. Miller, Robert Mitchell, Jack Simon, and Mae Fargo, of Associated Press; J. J. Fletcher, Herbert Starlight, Harry McDonnel, Joe and Frank Farina, Tilly Cohen, and Peter Sansone, of United Press; Harry Connors, of Brown Brothers; Otto L. Bettmann, of the Bettmann Archive; and Margaret Wilson.

As always, our deepest thanks to Dick Craven and Shirley Green and to Romana Javitz, head of the Picture Collection of the New York Public Library and her staff of picture librarians: Louise Leak, Franziska Gay Schacht, Marion Weithorn, Mary C. Magrish, Lenore Cowan, and Mrs. Delores Starks.

For his special technical assistance, our thanks to Maury Martin.

PROLOGUE

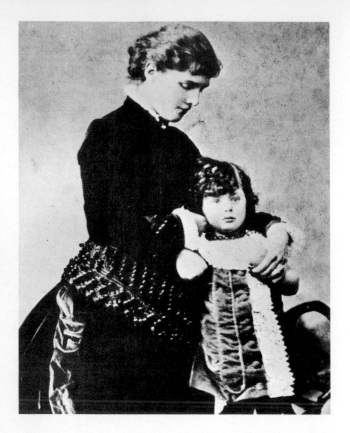

There were only two women in his life: his American mother . . .

. . . and his British wife.

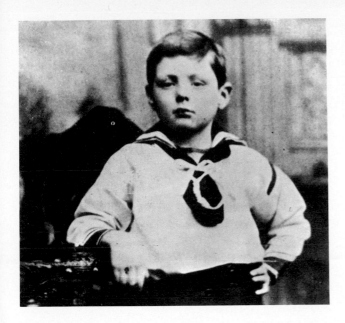

The small sailor who grew up to be . . .

. . . First Lord of the Admiralty

The son of a lord . . .

. . . the servant of his Queen

For King . . .

. . . and for country

"The human being is the only animal who can laugh . . .

. . . and cry."

"All babies look like me . . .   . . . and so do bulldogs."

A little boy's derby . . .

. . . became a great man's Homburg.

This German Kaiser was just an acquaintance . . .

. . . this American President was a friend.

Here was a man who . . .

. . . served six sovereigns.

He saw his country battered . . .

. . . but his enemy beaten.

The young carried him on their shoulders . . .

. . . the old carried him in their hearts.

Last in line in the lowest form at Harrow . . .

. . . man of the century

MAN
OF THE
CENTURY

Two years before the turn into the twentieth century, the British 21st Lancers in the Battle of Omdurman in Sudan ended an era with the last great cavalry charge. Traveling home to England afterwards, two young correspondents talked about the war, the British Empire, themselves. Doing most of the talking was the one with a freckled face, red hair, a thin mustache and a slight lisp—he had not only reported the cavalry charge, but had fought in it as a junior subaltern. So impressed was the other correspondent with his urgent, brilliant twenty-four-year-old companion, that he wrote a story about him called, "The Youngest Man in Europe," in which he said:

"In years he is a boy; in temperament he is also a boy; but in intention, in deliberate plan, purpose, adaptation of means to ends he is already a man . . .

"He is what he is by breeding. From his father he derives the hereditary aptitude for affairs, the grand style of entering upon them. From his American strain, he adds to this a keenness, a shrewdness, a half-cynical, personal ambition, a natural aptitude for advertisement and, happily, a sense of humor . . . qualities which might make him, almost at will, a great popular leader, a great journalist, or the founder of a great advertising business . . .

". . . He is ambitious and he is calculating; yet he is not cold. He has a queer, shrewd sense of introspection. . . . He has not studied to make himself a demagogue. He was born a demagogue and happens to know it.

". . . He has the twentieth century in his marrow . . .

"What will he become, who shall say? At the rate he goes, there will hardly be room for him in Parliament at thirty, or in England at forty."

This was written by G. W. Steevens of the London *Daily Mail.* The other correspondent, representing the London *Post,* was Winston Churchill.

The assessment was sound. Born at a time and in a country where youth was an unpardonable thing, Winston Leonard Spencer Churchill saw more of war at twenty-six as a soldier than half the generals of Europe did, became the most famous war correspondent of his time, later held more cabinet offices than any other man in English history ever held, and earned a Nobel prize for his own writing of history.

But, much more than all that, here was a man who made his own history, who bestrode "the narrow world like a Colossus," who may have boggled some big decisions but never niggled them, who had such sweep of style and spirit that he transformed his nation's time of trial into its finest hour, who grew old with the rare knowledge that he had made himself immortal while he was still alive.

During his later years, a child came up to him at a family party and asked him, "Are you the greatest man in the world?" Churchill answered brusquely, "Of course, now buzz off."

His own announced assessment of himself was more modest. "We are all worms," he said, "but I do believe I am a glowworm."

This is a man who was born only ten years after the Civil War. When William McKinley was President of the United States, Winston Churchill was in a Boer prison camp. When Theodore Roosevelt became President, Churchill was twenty-six, a prominent war hero, an emerging Member of Parliament and author of several celebrated books (and he had been a Rough Rider in Cuba two years before Roosevelt was). When President Woodrow Wilson was busy completing the Panama Canal, First Lord of the Admiralty Churchill already had prepared the British Navy for the looming war with Germany. And when Franklin D. Roosevelt had finished his first hundred days as President in 1933, and Adolf Hitler was busy becoming a naked fist of fascist force in the world, Winston Churchill was supposedly "an old man in retirement, politically finished."

And yet, the growth of his greatness was still on the horizon.

His first name, Winston, came from an early ancestor, a cavalier knight, the father of John Churchill, first Duke of Marlborough. His middle name, Leonard, came from his American grandfather, Leonard Jerome, a self-made millionaire who liked good horses, good-looking women and Gatling guns—and was also part-owner of *The New York Times.*

Churchill's genes had much of both breeds.

The young Winston hated school. Yet, at Harrow, where he was "last in line," he told another boy, "I shall be a greater man than you."

He almost didn't get into Sandhurst:

"If this aged, weary-souled Civil Service Commissioner had not asked this particular question about these cosines or tangents in their squared or even cubed condition which I happened to have learned scarcely a week before, I might have gone into the Church and preached orthodox sermons in a spirit of anxious contradiction to the age.

"I might have gone into the City and made a fortune. I might have gravitated to the Bar and persons might have been hanged through my defence. Anyhow the whole of my life would have been altered and I suppose would have altered a great many other lives."

At twenty-one, he said, "I am getting absurdly old." It seemed then that his fate was to be known as the son of a famous father. But he still had enough self-confidence to say, when giving a party for some young friends, that they, including himself, "in twenty years would control the destinies of the British Empire."

War was his zest, politics his zeal. Writing a novel called *Savrola*, Churchill said of his hero, "Ambition was the motive force and he was powerless to resist it. Vehement, high and daring was his cast of mind."

It sometimes made him almost insufferable. Elected to Parliament in 1900, he was called, "the spoiled child of the House." In a debate on the Boer War, he told his elders, "You can only read about it; I was there." Later, as the youngest member of the Cabinet, he was quoted as saying, "Sometimes I think I can carry the whole world on my shoulders." It made him, according to many, "one of the best-hated men in England."

After one of his early election defeats, when he was thirty-one, a critic said of him, "He has ridiculed those in high places, he has insulted his cousin and patron, the Duke. Without political friends, without the influence and money of the Marlborough family, he is a political nonentity."

Another noted critic, Frank Harris, wrote in an American magazine in 1917, "Winston Churchill is not democratic enough to be popular. He knows no foreign language, cannot even speak French. He has read scarcely at all, and outside of a smattering of history is outstandingly ignorant of the best that has been thought and said in the world. He has no inkling of the fact that simplicity is the hallmark of greatness in manners as in style. He has no suspicion that there are heights above him as mighty as the depths beneath.

"It appears that no great or original stroke of genius need be expected from him in any place.

"He is an excellent subaltern, capable, industrious . . . but not a pathfinder or a great leader of men."

In the House of Commons, some said of him that he was much like his father—brilliant but unstable, and a dangerous man with whom to work. Like his father, too, they predicted he would be old at forty, in his grave at forty-five.

Winston Churchill himself said, "We Churchills peg out early. I must make sure of my innings."

Noting all the critics, his aunt made a pithy point: "You see all of Winston's faults in the first half hour," she said. "You spend the rest of your life discovering his virtues."

His virtues were more than the fact that he turned pink when he tried to tell a lie, or that he had this strong tendency to swim against the stream. On becoming First Lord of the Admiralty, he tore up his identification pass, handed it to the doorman and said, "My face is my fortune."

But it was not his face. It was his courage.

"Courage," he had said, "is rightly esteemed the first of human qualities . . . because it is the quality which guarantees all others."

But it took more than courage to make "all the days good, each day better than the other." He needed help. "Life is a whole and luck is a whole," he said, "and no part of them can be separated from the rest."

The luck of his life was his two women: his mother and his wife. His American mother, the former Jennie Jerome of Brooklyn, who helped get him newspaper assignments, acted as agent to get his books published, influenced his reading, dined the whole list of British generals to get him transferred to the wars he wanted, helped him campaign in elections and, throughout her lifetime, always sat in the Distinguished Guest Box in Parliament whenever he made a speech.

His wife, Clementine Hozier, "the most beautiful girl in England," who mothered his five children, went where he went, served as his compass, his umbrella and, later, his cane. She took over in all emergencies, whether he was bored into silence at a big dinner, or when he told her, "You'll have to carve it, Clemmie; this goose was a friend of mine."

"If there was a decision to be made," said one of Churchill's secretaries, Phyllis Moir, "Mrs. Churchill was invariably consulted. Working with Mr. Churchill, I soon grew accustomed to the cry of 'Clemmie, Clemmie,' which seemed to ring through the apartment all day long."

And yet, he had an unchanged view of women in politics. During his younger days, when he still had a slight mustache, a suffragette wrote him that she liked his politics as little as his mustache. "Don't worry, madam," he wrote her. "You are not likely to come into contact with either." Years later, when Lady Astor was the first woman seated in Parliament, Churchill told her, "When you entered, I felt you had come upon me in my bath and I'd nothing to protect myself but the sponge."

His sense of humor in the House of Commons had a bite to it:

"Call that a maiden speech?" he once said. "That was a brazen hussy of a speech . . ."

When asked about another speech, he said, "Well, I thought it was very good. It must have been good, for it contained, as far as I know, all the platitudes known to the human race, with the possible exception of, 'Prepare to meet thy God,' and, 'Please adjust your dress before leaving.' "

And, of a haughty House Member, he said, "There, but for the grace of God, goes God."

"All the years that I have been in the House of Commons, I have always said to myself one thing: 'Do not interrupt.' I have never been able to keep to that resolution."

More important than his sense of humor was his sense of prescience. "The truth is inconvertible," he said in 1916. "Panic may resent it; ignorance may deride it; malice may distort it; but there it is."

He saw the coming of the First World War. He warned, but few listened. As First Lord of the Admiralty, he got the fleet ready, the oil reserves set, checked the thickness of the armor plate. The readied Navy helped win the war.

He saw the coming of the Second World War. Back in 1925, he wrote "Shall We Commit Suicide?," in which he preached preparedness. "Let it not be thought for a moment that the danger of another explosion in Europe is past." With Hitler's rise, he still believed a war was easily avoided by early firmness, without the firing of a single shot.

Instead, the British government adopted a policy of appeasement with Munich, and Churchill warned, "Each one hopes that if he feeds the crocodile enough, it will eat him last."

At a dinner at that time, somebody said that nothing was worse than war, and Churchill bristled. "Nothing is worse than war? Dishonor is worse than war. Slavery is worse than war."

Something that fits the tone of the time was a poem he remembered reading in *Punch* when he was about nine years old:

> Who is in charge of the clattering train?
> The axles creak and the couplings strain;
> And the pace is hot, and the points are near,
> And sleep has deadened the driver's ear;
> And the signals flash through the night in vain,
> For Death is in charge of the clattering train.

When war came, the train needed a new engineer and Winston Churchill became Prime Minister.

"Never give in," he once told the boys at Harrow, "never, never, never, never, in nothing great or small, large or petty—never give in except to convictions of honor and good sense. Never yield to force, never yield to the apparently overwhelming might of the enemy."

When Hitler threatened invasion of England, the unprepared British had to pull artillery pieces out of museums. Churchill made his speech "We shall fight them on the streets . . ." and, after he had finished, he covered the BBC microphone with his hand and added a postscript, "We shall beat them over the head with bottles—that's all we've got."

He was the "daring pilot in extremity, pleased with the dangers when the waves ran high." Years later, when somebody asked him what was his darkest hour, he said there wasn't any. "I loved every minute of it."

One of the "deeps within him" was his magic with words, his feeling for phrase. If the experts complained that he dropped his voice when he should raise it, that he sometimes lacked clarity, that he lisped, still his oratory had a power to it, his speech had a ring and a roll packed with the arrogance and spirit and splendor of Elizabethan language.

"Come, then: let us to the task, to the battle, to the toil—each to our part, each to our station. Fill the armies, rule the air, pour out the munitions, strangle the U-boats, sweep the mines, plough the land, build the ships, guard the streets, succor the wounded, uplift the downcast and honor the brave."

"His special gift is his moral quality," commented Walter Lippmann. "He draws men out of their meaner selves and fascinates them with greatness. The springs of greatness in a public man lie finally, as they do in Winston Churchill, in the conviction that he must serve truth and not opinion, that he must do what is right whether or not he is sure to succeed. That was how in the darkest hours of 1940 Churchill made the choice between honor and calculation. When none would calculate the future of Britain, he settled the issue on the ground of honor and of duty.

"This is the road to greatness."

When Lady Diana Cooper suggested to Churchill that the most important thing he had done was to give people courage, he said, "I never gave them courage. I was able to focus theirs."

He could focus this courage with a quip: After the fall of France, one French leader freely predicted that Great Britain also wouldn't last more than three weeks, that it would have its neck wrung like a chicken. Churchill remembered it, later quoted it, adding, "Some chicken . . ." As the laughter barely died away, he added, ". . . some neck." And the laughter exploded.

And when critics complained of Churchill's quick decision to aid Russia after Hitler had invaded the Soviets, Churchill said, "If Hitler invaded Hell, I would at least make a favorable reference to the Devil in the House of Commons."

Stalin toasted Churchill at Yalta as "this one man who led his country into war." Then Stalin turned to Franklin D. Roosevelt and added, "Not like you and I, who were pushed into war by an invasion."

F.D.R. was Churchill's fast friend. When F.D.R. died, Churchill said of him, "He was loved by millions. Inside and outside the United States. Hated, too, as who isn't who gets things done. I'll be hated. But I'm composed about it. It requires no resignation on my part. I'm sure it took none for Franklin."

With the end of the war in Europe, Churchill needed all his resignation because the British people held a general election and retired him from office.

"I am a child of the House of Commons," he had once said to an American Congress. "I was brought up in my father's house to believe in democracy. 'Trust the people' was his message. . . . In my country, in yours, public men are proud to be the servants of the state and would be ashamed to be its masters."

A newspaper quoted one man who said, "Well, 'e's 'ad a run for it." But an old lady was quoted as saying, "It won't be the same without him."

Churchill later said, "Any private ambitions I may have cherished in my younger days have been satisfied beyond my wildest dreams."

Yet he must have had qualms and questions when he looked ahead to retirement. Perhaps he even remembered something he had written in his novel *Savrola* about his hero:

"He could appreciate the delights of an artist, a life devoted to the search for beauty, or of sport, the keenest pleasure that leaves no sting behind. To live in a dreamy quiet and philosophic calm in some beautiful garden far from the noise of men and with every diversion that art and intellect could suggest, was, he felt, a more agreeable picture. And yet he knew that he could not endure it."

He did have his writing. "If Winston would give up politics and stick to writing," one critic had said, "he might be the most brilliant British historian since Macaulay." Churchill had his own reaction to this: "Writing a book was an adventure. To begin with, it was a toy, an amusement; then it became a mistress, and then a master, and then a tyrant."

What helped him most in writing was his almost encyclopedic memory. He could recite Shakespeare by the hour or pull out all the words to all the songs in a musical he once saw called *Lady Be Good*.

"I have tunes in my head," he once said, "for every war I have been to, and indeed for every critical or exciting phase of my life. Someday, when my ship comes home, I am going to have them all collected in a gramophone record, and then I will sit in a chair and smoke my cigar, while pictures and faces, moods and sensations long vanished return."

One such tune had this verse:

> Great white mother
> Far across the sea
> Ruler of Empire, may she ever be.
> Long may she reign, glorious and free.

Invited everywhere to speak, he said he was glad to talk about the past rather than peer into the future, "because I know more about the past than about the future." Yet, in Fulton, Missouri, it was Churchill looking into the grim future, saying, "From Stettin in the Baltic to Trieste in the Adriatic, an iron curtain has descended across the continent."

It was Churchill who said, long before most, "Africa is not a seat but a springboard." It was Churchill who predicted back in 1925, "Might not a bomb no bigger than an orange be found to possess a secret power . . . to blast a township at a stroke . . . guided automatically in flying machines by wireless or other rays, without a human pilot?"

And it was now Churchill who said, "The Dark Ages may return—the Stone Age may return on the gleaming wings of science; and what might now shower immeasurable material blessings upon mankind may even bring about its total destruction. Beware, I say! Time may be short."

But he added a note of hope: "As long as we have freedom, I am not afraid of the future."

He was in his middle seventies when his country's election swept him back into the office of Prime Minister. On the small stage of the modern world, the figure of Winston Churchill again seemed even more fabulous.

"As in a great castle which has long contended with Time, the mighty central mass of the donjon towered up intact, and seemingly everlasting," Churchill once had said, in reference to an old friend. Of Oliver Cromwell, Churchill had said, "Amid the ruins of every institution, social and political, which had hitherto guided the Island life, he towered up gigantic, glowing, indispensable." And in his novel Churchill had written of his hero, "And history, while . . . she notes his many errors, will yet deliberately pronounce that among the eminent men whose bones lie near his, scarcely one has left a more stainless and none a more splendid name."

All of his own words of others seem to fit facets of himself. But there are so many facets with so many "deeps."

One of the most stirring is a message he wrote several decades ago:

"Come on now, all you young men all over the world. You are needed more than ever now to fill the gap of a generation shorn by the war. You have not an hour to lose. You must take your places in Life's fighting line. Twenty to twenty-five! These are the years! Don't be content with things as they are. 'The earth is yours and the fulness thereof.' Enter upon your inheritance, accept your responsibilities. Raise the glorious flags again, advance them upon the new enemies, who constantly gather upon the front of the human army, and have only to be assaulted to be overthrown. Don't take No for an answer. Never submit to failure. Do not be fobbed off with mere personal success or acceptance. You will make all kinds of mistakes; but as long as you are generous and true, and also fierce, you cannot hurt the world or even seriously distress her. She was made to be wooed and won by youth. She has lived and thrived only by repeated subjugations."

He had said later, "I have not always been wrong about the future of events, and if you will permit me, I shall inscribe some of these words as my testament, because I should like to be held accountable for them in years which I shall not see."

A small boy named Roger Fabray recently sent the great man a letter:

"DEAR SIR WINSTON,

I send you my week's spending money (20 cents) for a birthday present. When I grow up, I hope to be just like you."

Somebody should tell Roger Fabray that the odds are against it, the odds are very much against it. Or, to quote another Englishman, famous in another age, we "shall not look upon his like again."

But if we do, if someday there springs another giant of greatness, another man of the century who fills a world's need in time of crisis, then perhaps we will be able to trace back some of the same seeds of quality: the stubborn courage, the wide range of mind, the soaring spirit.

It was Winston Churchill's American grandfather, Leonard Jerome, who told his daughter Jennie, "I have given you all I have. Pass it on."

Who in this century—speaking to the promise of tomorrow's greatness—who can say to the world, with greater satisfaction than that of Winston Leonard Spencer Churchill, "I have given you all I have. Pass it on."

First of his ancestors to come to America (1688), from the Isle of Wight, was a sergeant of a train band, Timothy Jerome (and he spelled it several different ways).

"My mother was American," Winston Churchill said, "and my ancestors were officers in Washington's Army. So I myself am an English-speaking union . . ."

Mother

2 A. Jennie Jerome, b. Brooklyn, N. Y., 9 Jan. 1854, m. at the British Embassy, Paris, 15 Apr. 1874 to Lord Randolph Churchill, m. 2 Lieut. George Cornwallis West, m. 3 Montagu Porch, d. 28 June 1921.

Parents

2 B. Clarissa Hall, b. 16 July 1825, Palmyra, Wayne Co., N. Y., m. 5 Apr. 1849, Palmyra, d. Apr. 1895 at Tunbridge Wells, Eng., bur. Green-Wood Cem. Brooklyn, N. Y., 13 July 1895. noted beauty of her day. Called Clarissa in girlhood, Clara after marriage.

1 B. Leonard Walter Jerome, b. 3 Nov. 1817, Pompey, Onondaga Co., N. Y., d. 3 Mar. 1891, Brighton, Eng., bur. 5 Aug. 1891, Green-Wood Cem., Brooklyn, N. Y. Lived at Pompey, Palmyra, Rochester, Brooklyn, New York. Publisher, business man, financier, sportsman. B. A. Union 1840.

Grand Parents

4 C. Clarissa Willcox, b. 10 Sept. 1796, Palmyra, N. Y., m. 24 Dec. 1817, Palmyra, d. July 1827, Palmyra, a few days after birth of her sixth daughter.

3 C. Ambrose Hall, b. 29 Aug. 1774, Laneboro, Berkshire Co. Mass. Removed to Palmyra 1818 from Williamstown, Mass. d. 14 Oct 1827, Palmyra. A member of The Assembly N. Y. State 1826.

2 C. Aurora Murray, b. 18 Jan. 1785, Canaan, Columbia Co., N. Y., m. 18 Mar. 1807, Pompey, N. Y., d. 6 Apr. 1867, N. Y. City. She and Isaac Jerome were mar. 59 yrs.

1 C. Capt. Isaac Jerome, b. 26 Oct. 1786, Charlton, Saratoga Co., N. Y. Lived at Pompey, Manlius, Palmyra, N. Y. Lieut. Grenadiers 98th Regt., Onondaga Co. Militia 1815, Capt. 1819, d. 20 July 1866, Syracuse, N. Y.

2 G. Grand Parents

1 D. Lieut. Aaron Jerome. b. 3 Nov. 1728, Wallingford, Conn., m. 19 Nov. 1749 Wallingford. Removed to Stockbridge, Mass. serg. Berkshire Co. Militia in Rev. Removed to N. Y. state abt 1785. d. Onondaga Co. N. Y., 1796.

2 E. Lucy Foster, b. 28 Mar. 1732, Wallingford, Conn.

1 E. Samuel Jerome.

2 D. Elizabeth Ball. b. Meriden section, Wallingford, Conn., 4 Dec. 1764, m. 14 Apr. 1802, Pompey, N. Y. Lieut. 1796, Lieut. Col. John Ball's Regt. Saratoga Co. Militia. Lived Stockbridge, Mass., Charlton and Pompey, N. Y.

2 D. Elizabeth Ball. b. 1 Nov. 1739, Granville, Mass., m. 2. 14 Oct. 1804, Rev. Joshua Johnson, m. 3. Dr. Axel Ensworth. Living in 1838.

3 E. Major Libbeus Ball. b. 11 Nov. 1739, Granville, Mass., m. Granville, 20 May 1762 (int.) Capt. 4th Mass. Regt. 1775. Major 1777, wounded, retired from service 1782. Removed Ballston and Pompey, N. Y., d. 1806.

4 E. Thankful Stow.

3 D. Lieut. Reuben Murray. b. 17 Feb. 1743/4, E. Guilford, Conn., m. 1. 1766, Sarah Guthrie, m. 2. Mrs. Sarah (Knickerbocker) Griffin, d. 26 Nov. 1810, Pompey, N. Y., Lieut. in Col. Burrall's Conn. Regt. and in Cols. Whiting, and Van Alystine's, N. Y., Regts. in Revolution.

5 E. Jehiel Murray. b. 28 Mar. 1708, E. Guilford, Conn. to Kent, Litchfield Co. 1744. Reuben Murray were men of fine presence and considerable property.

6 E. Mary Way, b. 9 Aug. 1715, d. 12 Oct. 1806.

4 D. Sarah Guthrie. b. 30 Apr. 1744. Woodbury, Conn. d. 1792.

7 E. John Guthrie. In Durham, Conn., cir. 1719, a colonist from Scotland. Removed to Kent, Litchfield Co., abt. 1743, m. 1 June 1727, Abigail Coe, m. 2 Susannah ——. He d. July 1756, b. prob. abt. 1700.

8 E. Abigail Coe, b. 11 Nov. 1702, at Stratford, Conn., d. 23 Mar. 1747.

6 D. Mehitable Beach. b. July 1749, North Stratford, Conn., d. 17 Sept. 1807, Albany, N. Y., age 58.

9 E. Thomas Hall. b. 10 May 1712, Wallingford, Conn., m. 24 Apr. 1734, Wallingford. d. 1800 at Wallingford.

5 D. Ambrose Hall. b. Wallingford, Conn. 3 Feb. 1735, an original proprietor and settler of Lanesboro, Mass. in Capt. Newell's Co., Col. Symon's Regt. called 1777. d. 29 Aug. 1800, Lanesboro.

10 E. Lydia Curtis, b. 20 Mar. 1714, Wallingford, Conn. d. 24 Sept. 1777.

7 D. David Willcox. b. 10 Jan. 1763 in Old Dartmouth, Bristol Co., Mass., m. abt. 1787. in Palmyra, Wayne Co. N. Y. in Apr. 1791, d. Macedon, Wayne Co., N. Y. 23 Aug. 1838. A blacksmith and farmer.

11 E. John Beach. b. 8 May 1718, Stratford, Conn., m. 23 Aug. 1748, Kent, Conn., d. 25 Mar. 1805, Monroe Center, Conn. Lived at North Stratford (Monroe).

12 E. Rebecca Berry, b. 9 July 1749, Tolland, Conn.

13 E. William Willcox. b. 8 Aug. 1739, Dartmouth, Mass., m. 2 Jan. 1760 (int.) Dartmouth, d. after 10 Sept. 1782, when named in mother's will. A blacksmith.

8 D. Anna Baker. g. g. Macedon, N. Y., states b. Nova Scotia, 27 May 1761, d. 28 Dec. 1813.

14 E. Sarah Smith, b. 27 Apr. 1741, Dartmouth.

3 G. Grand Parents

1 F. Timothy Jerome, b. cir. 1688. Appears in Windham, Conn., 1713. In Wallingford, Conn., 1717. Sergeant of train band, d. 23 Feb. 1749/50, well to do man.

2 F. Abigail ——, m. 2. Jacob Deming, d. 18 Nov. 1771 in 83d yr.

3 F. Thomas Foster, m. Sept. 1727, Wallingford, Conn., d. there, 1756.

4 F. Mary Clark, b. 8 May 1703, New Haven, Conn., d. 5 Apr. 1776.

5 F. Jonathan Ball, b. 1692, m. 11 Nov. 1729, d. cir. 1778. Lived at Granville, Mass. Olde Genealogy states he was married 2 Dec. 1726.

6 F. Elizabeth Olds, b. 19 Mar. 1698/9.

7 F. Elikalim Stow, b. 2 Mar. 1708, Middletown, Conn., m. 13 Dec. 1732. Removed to Granville, Mass. abt. 1760, m. 2. Catharine ——, d. 19 Aug. 1789.

8 F. Lydia Miller, bap. 17 Feb. 1711, Middletown, Conn., d. 27 May 1761.

9 F. Jonathan¹ Murray, appears in E. Guilford, Conn., 1685, prob. a colonist from Scotland. m. 17 July 1688, d. 27 Aug. 1747, æ 82.

10 F. Ann Bradley, b. 16 Nov. 1669, d. 1 June 1749.

11 F. George Way, b. Lyme, Conn., before 1696, removed to Lebanon, Conn., later to Guilford, and back to Lyme, m. 19 July 1713 at Lebanon.

12 F. Lydia Sprague.

13 F. Capt. John Coe, b. 10 May 1656, Stratford, Conn., m. 20 Dec. 1682, Capt. 1709. In service in Queen Anne's war. Deputy to Gen. Court of Conn., g. a Stratford, d. 19 Apr. 1741.

14 F. Mary Hawley, b. 16 July 1668, Stratford, Conn., d. 9 Sept. 1731.

15 F. Thomas Hall, b. 17 July 1676, Wallingford, Conn., m. 26 Apr. 1711, d. 23 June 1762, Wallingford, Conn.

16 F. Abigail Atwater, b. 17 Oct. 1685, Wallingford, Conn.

17 F. Nathaniel Curtis, b. 14 Nov. 1667, Wallingford, Conn., m. 1 'Sarah Hall', m. 2 29 July 1702, Sarah How. Sergt. Wallingford train band, d. 4 Mar. 1763.

18 F. Sarah How, b. 30 Oct. 1675, Wallingford, d. 4 Jan. 1740.

19 F. Ebenezer Beach, b. 14 Sept. 1692, Stratford, Conn., m. 28 Dec. 1715, Stratford, d. there Jan. 1776.

20 F. Mehitable Gibson, b. 28 Aug. 1693, Boston, Mass. She was living in Milford, Conn., when married.

21 F. Capt. Nathaniel Berry, b. May 1692, Portsmouth, N. H., m. cir. 1722. Removed from Tolland, Conn., 1738, original prop. of Kent, Ensign 1738, Lieut. 1745, Capt. 1750. Prob. d. Kent, Conn., abt. 1770.

22 F. Rebecca ——, 7 children, b. Tolland, 4 in Kent.

23 F. William Willcox, b. 22 Nov. 1711, Dartmouth, Mass., m. 8 Feb. 1732/3, d. Dartmouth, abt. 1742. A blacksmith.

24 F. Dorothy Allen, b. cir. 1713, granted adm. on husband's est. 18 Oct. 1743, she having six small children, eldest being ten. Will signed 19 Sept. 1782, pro. 30 Nov. 1782.

25 F. Eleazar Smith, b. 11 May 1713, Dartmouth, Mass., m. cir. 1740. Many time in Dartmouth land recs. down to 1768.

26 F. Meribah ——.

4 G. Grand Parents

Con't 5 G. Bartholomew Foster, mother's name not known.

Con't 7 G. Samuel Clark.
Con't 8 G. Mary Brown.

Con't 9 G. Capt. Jonathan Ball, mother's name not known.

Con't 11 G. Dr. Robert Olds.
Con't 12 G. Elizabeth (Atchison) Lam

Con't 13 G. Nathaniel Stow.
Con't 14 G. Sarah Sumner.

Con't 15 G. Benjamin Miller.
Con't 16 G. Mercy Bassett.

Con't 19 G. Nathan Bradley.
Con't 20 G. Hester Griswold.

Con't 21 G. George Way.
Con't 22 G. Susannah Nest.

Con't 23 G. Lieut. John Sprague, mother's name not known.

Con't 25 G. Robert Coe.
Con't 26 G. Hannah Mitchell.

Con't 31 G. Joseph Hawley.

Con't 33 G. Thomas Hall.
Con't 34 G. Grace Watson.

Con't 35 G. John Atwater.
Con't 36 G. Abigail Mansfield.

Con't 37 G. Thomas Curtis.
Con't 38 G. Mary Merriman.

Con't 39 G. Zachariah How.
Con't 40 G. Sarah Gilbert.

Con't 41 G. John Beach.
Con't 42 G. Hannah Staples.

Con't 43 G. William Gibson.
Con't 44 G. Hannah Philpen.

Con't 45 G. Nathaniel Berry.
Con't 46 G. Elizabeth Philbrick.

Con't 49 G. Daniel Willcox, mother's name not known.

Con't 51 G. Benjamin Allen.
Con't 52 G. Deborah Russell.

Con't 53 G. Gershom Smith.
Con't 54 G. Rebecca Ripley.

Timothy carefully left behind a recorded inventory of his estate, which included, among many other things, a large calf, a churn, two fine shirts, a silk handkerchief, a small iron kettle, a jackknife, a dough trough and a punch bowl.

	£	s	d
Small Ditto 10/. Large pewter bowl 3/ Ditto 10/	00	00	0
inking Glaſs 10/. tin Cullindr 06/. Several things	01	04	0
Looking Glaſs 5/. Case of pottles 10/. 3 Quart tills 1/2		01	0
Large pottle 2/ 3 ¾ pint pottles 1/6. Ditto 2/ Ditto	00	19	6
ials 3/. Ditto 2/ Hour Glaſs 6/. Ditto 1/ & four tins 02		13	00
ta 2/. 4 Milk pans 10/ 2 Erthen punch bowls 5/	01	03	00
than pitchers 6/. 3 Erthen platters 6/ Ditto large 3/	00	15	00
Erthan plates 1/6 Ditto 3/. 3 Erthan pots 10/ Ditto 2/	01		06
& pudding pan 2/6. Bason 1/6. pint mug 16 pot 16	00	07	00
oringers 3/. Erthan Salt Cellar 3/	00	02	0
rge Braſs Cittle 2/ Ditto 3/. Ditto 2/5	06	5	0
ming pan 5/6. poſane pot 3/ Iron skiit 1/6	04	10	00
small Iven Cittle 3/. a Roaſting Iron 1/3	02	05	00
vid Iron 1/9. Cleeper 6/ trammel 3/. Ditto 16	03	06	00
pare of tongs 1/8 fire peel 2/ Small tongs 1/0	02	18	00
rge Iron Cittle 2/ a Large trenpot 2/	12	00	0
pare of Andirons 2/5 fruing pan 15 Candle Stick 3/	02	06	0
pare of Shears 1/6 4 Case knives & forks 2/	01	01	06
knife 3/ 2 old Case knives 5/	00	08	00
Small Cellers 2/. old pail 2/. Ditto 3/. Ditto 6/ Ditto 4/	02	06	00
d pail 1/6. 2 trays 2/ 2 bowls 2/ wooden platters	00	15	06
ooden bowls poone 1/2/ 1 Erthen pot 5/ 3 branders 3/	01	05	00
Diſh 2/ Skiming Diſh and wooden diſh 1/6	00	07	06
meal Sive 3/ Dough trough 2/ Duch Real 2/	02	14	00
reat wheals 2/5 2 pare of old Cards one 1/6	02	16	06
other 3/ Ditto 1/6 a Large Dry Caſk 2/ Ditto 2/	04	09	06
turn 18/ a Large Caſk 1/10 Barrel 2/ Ditto 2/	04	03	00
d Caſk 1/10. Ditto 2/ Ditto 2/ Meat barrel 1/6	03	03	00
Caſk 2/ Linnen wheal 2/ Redland Jack 10/	01	18	00
Loom 4/. 2 old Caſk 1/10. 2 Corn baskets 1/4	02	18	00
to 3/ Ditto 3/ Ditto 2/ Ditto 3/ Ditto 2/6 fine Baſh	01	03	06
to 4/ Ditto 2/6. Ditto 3/6. Ditto 2/6 Great Chair 10/	01	07	06
lack Chairs 2/ Great Chair 10/ plain Chairs 3/	05	15	00
old plain table 1/2/ Cheſt of two drawers 8/	08	12	00
nd table 4/ Cheſt with one Draw 2/10	10	10	00
ain Cheſt 2/10. 2/ of Flax 8-10-6 Clever 1/10	12	10	06
meal bags 2/8 an old Saddle 2/ bridle 1/3	06	13	00
nd Saw 2/ Inch auger 2/ Chisel 10/	03	10	00
	146	12	6

IN MEMORY OF
THE FIRST SETTLERS OF THE
TOWN OF MERIDEN, WHO WERE
BURIED WITHIN & NEAR THIS
INCLOSURE & WHOSE NAMES
SO FAR AS KNOWN ARE
INSCRIBED ON THIS
MONUMENT.

THE MEETING HOUSE
IN WHICH THEY WORSHIPED &
THE FIRST ERECTED IN THE
TOWN STOOD ABOUT 50 RODS WEST
OF THIS MEMORIAL.

Timothy Jerome settled in Connecticut, was buried in an Indian cemetery high on Buckwheat Hill overlooking much of the land he owned.

Out of these roots came Leonard Jerome, a figure fabulous even in an era of fabulous figures. Twice wiped out of a fortune totaling an estimated ten million dollars, Leonard Jerome served as the American consul in Trieste (the youngest man in our foreign service at that time); he was a part-owner of *The New York Times* and the "father of the American turf." During the Civil War, when a rioting crowd threatened to storm the *Times*, Jerome mounted a new-fangled Gatling gun to face and quiet the crowd. Thirty years later, at the age of seventy-two, he accepted a circus strong man's challenge and knocked him senseless.

ABOVE. Jerome loved horses, drove up Fifth Avenue in New York City in the first four-in-hand the street had ever seen. BELOW. He started the first three race tracks, loaned his name to this one. His own horse, "Kentucky," never lost a race, and Jerome built a stable in town before he built his house. When the first American polo match was played at Jerome Park in 1876, Leonard Jerome couldn't play, because of a strain he had gotten that week in weight-lifting. He was then fifty-eight.

TOP. Over his huge town stable, Jerome built a private theater, and the stable itself often served as a setting for some of Jerome's fancy-dress balls. One of them featured two flowing fountains, one with cologne, the other with champagne. CENTER. Female society fascinated Leonard Jerome—especially Jenny Lind, the noted singer for whom Jerome built a theater. He even named his daughter after her. Mrs. Jerome, an understanding wife, told one of her husband's women admirers, "I don't blame you. I know how irresistible he is." BOTTOM. Mrs. Jerome, the former Clara Hall, a noted beauty of her day, came from Palmyra, New York. On her mother's side, some kin claimed blood relationship with the nearby Iroquois Indians.

29

ABOVE. Famous among the Iroquois orators of the time was Sa-go-ye-wat-ha, also known as "Red Jacket." BELOW. The Iroquois near Palmyra lived in this kind of "long house."

30

But it was in Brooklyn, New York, at 426 Henry Street, that the Leonard Jeromes lived and their daughter Jennie was born. (It was in Brooklyn, too, that Mr. and Mrs. Leonard Jerome were both buried.)

There were soon three Jerome sisters (Jennie, extreme left). One sister later died. But, while the girls were still infants, Leonard Jerome swept his whole family from Brooklyn to Trieste, where he was made American consul. Until she was six years old, Jennie hardly spoke anything but Italian. Their mother's favorite comment about them was, "The girls are just like Leonard—never, never tired."

Back in New York, they moved into a much
fancier house, on Twenty-sixth Street. One
of Jennie's earliest memories was of the time
their house was draped in black after the
assassination of President Abraham Lincoln.

TOP. She also remembered the many costume balls, especially one in which she dressed as a *vivandière* . . .

RIGHT. . . . and the Grand Ball at the New York Academy of Music for the Prince of Wales.

LEFT. Their mother took the girls back to Europe, into the glow and glitter of a social whirl. "One would think all these activities wear her out," Mrs. Jerome wrote her husband. "They wear me out." And her husband answered, "Jennie has so much energy, she should have been a boy."

But she hardly looked like a boy. In France, Napoleon III took her boating. Then there was a party for visiting Russian royalty aboard a cruiser anchored off Cowes, and Jennie Jerome met Randolph Churchill. They sat out some dances, and she later said that he impressed her because he was the only one there who talked to her intelligently. ABOVE. Soon after he met Jennie, Randolph Churchill remembered turning to a friend to say, "There is my future wife." Three days later, he proposed marriage; she accepted. Then Randolph wrote his father:

I must not any longer keep you in ignorance of a very important step I have taken—one which will undoubtedly influence very strongly all my future life.

I met, soon after my arrival at Cowes, a Miss Jeanette Jerome, the daughter of an American lady who has lived for some years in Paris and whose husband lives in New York. I passed most of my time at Cowes in her (Jeanette's) society, and before leaving asked her if she loved me well enough to marry me; and she told me she did. I do not think that if I were to write pages I could give you any idea of the strength of my feelings and affection and love for her; all I can say is that I love her better than life itself. . . .

I know of course you will be very much surprised. . . .

I now write you to . . . ask you whether you will be able to increase my allowance to some extent to put me in the position to ask Mrs. Jerome to let me become her daughter's future husband. Mr. Jerome is a gentleman who is obliged to live in New York to look after his business. I do not know what it is.

. . . In the last year or so I feel I have lost a great deal of what energy and ambition I possessed, and an idle and comparatively useless life has at times appeared to me to be the pleasantest; but if I were married to her whom I have told you about, if I had a companion, such as she would be, I feel sure, to take an interest in one's prospects and career, and to encourage me to exertions and to doing something towards making a name for myself, I think I might become, with the help of Providence, all and perhaps more than you had ever wished and hoped for me.

Jennie's father didn't much like her marrying the son of a lord, but Randolph's father was more vehement and called the idea, ". . . hasty, rash, headstrong, inconsidered, impulsive. You must return to England by the next boat." The final compromise was that Randolph first run for the parliamentary seat from Woodstock, the family borough, and then marry.

Randolph then won the election and won his bride.

IN THIS HOUSE IN JANUARY 1850 WAS BORN
JENNIE JEROME
LATER LADY RANDOLPH CHURCHILL

SHE WAS THE MOTHER OF
THE RT. HON. WINSTON SPENCER CHURCHILL
PRIME MINISTER OF GREAT BRITAIN
AND
STAUNCH FRIEND OF THE UNITED STATES

THIS PLAQUE IS ERECTED AS A MEMORIAL TO LADY CHURCHILL
TO EVIDENCE THE ESTEEM AND AFFECTION
IN WHICH HER SON IS HELD
BY THE PEOPLE OF THIS COMMUNITY

DEDICATED IN MARCH 1952

Her coat of arms was to be a plaque in Brooklyn . . .

Quartering's Crest and Supporters of
JOHN first DUKE of MARLBOROUGH.

And his had a motto, "Faithful but unfortunate."

But his heritage included the blood and bone of English history.

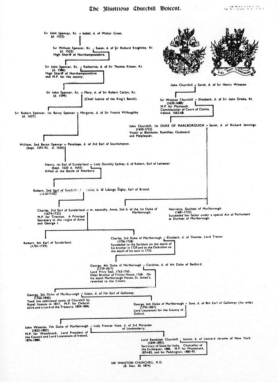

The Illustrious Churchill Descent.

The first Duke of Marlborough commanded the English armies for Queen Anne, fought France in ten campaigns, never fought a battle he did not win, never beseiged a fortress he did not take. Probably his greatest victory was the Battle of Blenheim, when he broke the French line with a cavalry attack.

Some two centuries after Marlborough's death, Winston Churchill wrote a four-volume biography of his distinguished ancestor, and quoted him liberally in the House of Commons: "As the great Marlborough said . . ."

Comparing the two men, one critic saw some qualities in common: ". . . perhaps his courage, his warlike tastes, much of his intellect and no little of his faculty for espousing new causes and discarding old ones."

ABOVE. If there was ever a woman to match a man, it was the first Marlborough's Duchess Sarah. Some say she not only ruled her roost, but occasionally helped run the British Empire. As Queen Anne's closest advisor, she was even credited by some with masterminding the final decision to make war on France.   BELOW. One poet wrote of her: "Who with herself, as others from her birth, Finds all her life one warfare on earth."

Grateful Queen Anne presented the Duke and Duchess with Blenheim Palace. It cost more than a million dollars to build—some 320 rooms set on 2,700 acres and soon filled with the treasures of the world.

Alexander Pope wrote of it:

The council chamber for debate
And all the rest are rooms of state.
"Thanks, sir," cried I, "'Tis very fine,
But where d'ya sleep, or where d'ya dine?
I find by all you have been telling,
That 'tis a house but not a dwelling."

Generations later, during an election campaign, Churchill spoke to sixty thousand people in front of Blenheim. Before the speech, he walked through the palace with Gerald O'Brien, seemed caught again by the spell of its history, its thousand-year-old oak trees. Then, suddenly, he turned and said, "O'Brien, has this old ruin got bathroom facilities for all these people?"

ABOVE. Blenheim became the home of Randolph's father, the seventh Duke of Marlborough. Randolph's mother, the former Lady Frances Anne Emily Vane, eldest daughter of the third Marquis of Londonderry.

One of eight children, Randolph was sent away to school at age eight, promptly cut his name into his new desk and reported home that his teacher had called him "a little blackguard." As he grew older, Randolph was noted for his vehemence of speech, his love of sport and horses, his deep interest in reading and history.

ABOVE. During his election campaigns, Randolph's wife, Jennie, campaigned hard for him, tramping the slums of London with her mother, asking its voters, "Please vote for my husband. I shall be so unhappy if you don't." But her husband made little early impact on the House of Commons. They said his temper matched his memory. Once, on a bet, he supposedly read through a page of Gibbon's *Decline and Fall of the Roman Empire,* shut the book and recited the whole page, word for word, without an error. "When I feel cross and angry," he once wrote his wife, "I read Gibbon, whose profound philosophy and easy though majestic writing soon quiets me down."

His son Winston later wrote of him, "Lord Randolph was of the temper that gallops until it falls."

And his American father-in-law sized him up: "Frail but fiery . . . Jennie is wonderful for him—he draws on her strength." BELOW. The new bride was not immediately happy about her social position. "The fact is, I loathe living here," she wrote home. "It's no use disguising it, the Duchess hates me for what I am—perhaps a little prettier and more attractive than her daughters."

But she hired an excellent French cook, entertained everybody from Prime Minister Disraeli to the Prince of Wales and even received word that, "The Queen thought you so handsome."

Lord D'Abernon thought so too. He described his first impression of her: ". . . a dark, lithe figure . . . radiant, translucent, intense. A diamond star in her hair, her favorite ornament—its luster dimmed by the flashing glory of her eyes. More of the panther than of the woman in her look, but with a cultivated intelligence unknown to the jungle. Her courage not less great than that of her husband—fit mother for descendants of the great Duke."

Her son Winston years later made this assessment: "My mother shone for me like an evening star. I loved her dearly, but at a distance."

ABOVE. Blenheim Palace was famous for its costume balls, and once she went as Empress Theodosia. BELOW. At another ball there, she suddenly excused herself in the midst of the dancing, raced through the Blenheim library, probably the longest room in England, a quarter of a mile of red carpet of the longest corridor in the country, until she reached the ladies' cloakroom.

The cloakroom was a small room on the ground floor, that once belonged to the first Duke's chaplain. Now it was filled with velvet capes and feather boas. And, there, in this huge palace which had held the history of a thousand years, the courts of Saxon, Norman and Plantaganet kings, a lady from Brooklyn gave birth, prematurely, to a boy she named Winston Leonard Spencer Churchill.

Nº. 28,176.

BIRTHS.

On the 30th Nov., at Blenheim Palace, the Lady RANDOLPH CHURCHILL, prematurely, of a son.

On the 7th Oct., at Rangoon, the wife of HALKETT F. JACKSON, Esq., Lieut. and Adjutant 67th Regt., of a daughter.

On the 20th Oct., at Bombay, the wife of Capt. G. W. OLDHAM, R.E., of a son.

On the 27th Oct., at Ranchi, Chota Nagpore, the wife of Capt. NINIAN LOWIS, B.S.C., Assistant Commissioner, of a daughter.

On the 6th Nov., 1874, at Belgaum, India, the wife of J. CHARLES M. PIGOTT, Esq., Lieut. 66th Regt., of a daughter.

On the 20th Nov., at Marlborough-terrace, Roath, Cardiff, the wife of THOMAS J. ALLEN, of a daughter.

On the 21st Nov., the wife of POYNTZ WRIGHT, M.R.C.S.E., of a daughter.

On the 22d Nov., at South-hill-park, Hampstead, the wife of ALBERT STRAUBE, of a son.

On the 26th Nov., at Wolfang, Queensland, Australia, the wife of HENRY DE SATGÉ, Esq., of a son.

TOP. A family friend had this comment on the new baby: "Interesting breeding. Stamina always goes through the dam, and pace, through the sire." Another friend looked back years later and added, "From his father he inherited a reckless indifference to risk. From his mother he derived a baffling adaptability to circumstances." BOTTOM. Winston's first letter.

My dear mama
I am so glad
you are coming
to see us I had
such a nice

bathe in the
sea to day.
love to papa
your loving
winston

ABOVE. Randolph moved his family to Ireland, where he served as secretary to his father, the newly appointed Lord-Lieutenant of Ireland. They lived adjacent to this viceregal lodge in Phoenix Park.

"When does one first begin to remember?" said Winston Churchill. "When do the waving lights and shadows of dawning consciousness cast their print upon the mind of a child?

"I remember my grandfather, the Viceroy, unveiling the Lord Gough statue in 1878. A great black crowd, scarlet soldiers on horseback, string pulling away a brown shiny sheet, the old Duke, the formidable grandpapa, talking loudly to the crowd.

"I recall even a phrase he used: '. . . and with a withering volley, he shattered the enemy's line . . .'

"I quite understood that he was talking about war and fighting and that 'a volley' meant what the black-coated soldiers used to do with loud bangs in the Phoenix Park where I was taken for my morning walks. This, I think, is my first coherent memory." BELOW. His mother (seated, center) called him the "naughtiest small boy in the world." Other family members called him "a troublesome boy" and "that little upstart." A female cousin remembered him more kindly as "ardent and vital."

Winston poured out all his troubles to his one confidante, his nurse, Mrs. Everest. She was the one, on a family visit to Paris when he was an infant, who had wheeled him in his perambulator up the street she called "the shams Elizee." She was the one who gave him his lasting love of Kent as "the garden of England." She was the one who prepared him for reading with a book called *Reading Without Tears*. For Winston, the book did not justify the title.

But much worse than letters, were figures. "Letters, after all, had only to be known," he said, "and when they stood together in a certain way, one recognized their formation and that it meant a certain word or sound which one uttered when pressed sufficiently. But the figures were tied into all sorts of tangles and did things to one another which it was extremely difficult to forecast with complete accuracy."

When a governess came to give advanced lessons, Winston hid in the shrubbery for hours. But of Mrs. Everest, he later remarked, "If there be any, as I trust there are some, who rejoice that I live, to that dear and excellent woman their gratitude is due."

ABOVE. They nicknamed him "Coppertop" because of his red hair. His busy mother saw him as a little boy susceptible to colds. His busier father, who had become Secretary of State for India, saw his boy even more seldom, but did drop off a copy of *Treasure Island,* which Winston "devoured" with delight. Teachers noted that he eagerly read only what interested him, learned only when his imagination was stirred. Otherwise he loved playing with his toys in his nursery: a real steam engine, a magic lantern and a private army of 1,500 soldiers.

"I was happy as a child with my toys in my nursery," he said. "I have been happier every year since I became a man." BELOW. His toy soldiers were all of one size, all British, organized as an infantry division with a cavalry brigade and he was constantly arranging them in intricate battles. One day his father paid a formal visit of inspection, spent twenty minutes surveying the scene, the troops correctly formed for attack, and he smiled and asked his son whether he would like to go into the Army. "I thought it would be splendid to command an Army," said Winston, "so I said 'Yes' at once: and immediately I was taken at my word.

"For years I thought my father with his experience and flair had discerned in me the qualities of military genius. But I was told later that he had only come to the conclusion that I was not clever enough to go to the Bar. However that may be, the toy soldiers turned the current of my life."

ABOVE. His younger brother John (left) learned from Winston how to use a pea-shooter. But Winston was now more and more in school, which he hated. Discussing school as the "grey patch on my life," he said, "I would rather have been apprenticed as a bricklayer's mate or run errands as a messenger boy. It would have been more natural, it would have taught me more and I should have done it better." BELOW. His mother worried about her son Winston (right) and his inability to adjust at school. "It's very difficult to tell what goes on in his mind," she wrote her father. Mr. Jerome, himself a prime nonconformist, answered quickly, "Let him be. Boys get good at what they find they shine at."

Winston soon showed something he seemed to shine at. "I am getting on in drawing," he wrote her, "and like it very much. I am going to begin shading in sepia."

In his examinations for entrance into Harrow, twelve-year-old Winston complained that he would have willingly displayed his knowledge in history, poetry and writing essays, but the examiners insisted on exposing his ignorance in Latin and mathematics. He couldn't answer a single question on the Latin paper, handed in a blank page with some ink blots.

"It was from these slender indications of scholarship that Dr. Welden drew the conclusion that I was worthy to pass into Harrow. It was very much to his credit. It showed that he was a man capable of looking beneath the surface of things."

ABOVE. The boy on the highest step was the last boy in the lowest form. Not only did he refuse to absorb anything that didn't interest him, but he broke most of Harrow's rules (such as not keeping dogs in one's apartment) and picked up a reputation for bravery with "backchat." The Headmaster once called him in for reprimand, told him, "I have every grave reason to be displeased with you." Winston quickly answered, "And I, sir, have every grave reason to be displeased with you."

It didn't help his school reputation when he brought up his nurse, Mrs. Everest, and marched arm in arm with her up High Street. One of his classmates later said, "I only wish I had had the courage as a boy to bring my old nurse to see the school, as he did."

He won the public-school fencing championship, could recite whole scenes from Shakespeare and 1,200 lines from Macaulay's *Lays of Ancient Rome* without a mistake, edited the *Harrovian* and anonymously wrote for it. But they still kept him in the lowest form three times as long as anybody else. While his classmates went on to learn Latin and Greek, Winston got three times as much English, learning it thoroughly. "Thus I got into my bones the essential structure of the ordinary English sentence—which is a noble thing." Later he said he would let clever boys learn Latin as an honor, Greek as a treat, but the only thing he would whip them for was an ignorance of English. "I would whip them hard for that," he said.

His father was then Chancellor of the Exchequer, and visitors looked for him in the passing line of students. He overheard some say, "Why, he's the last of all!"

BELOW. Before he entered Harrow, Winston had a dinner for some of his young friends, where he told them blithely, "Someday I'm going to rule England." After he left Harrow, he limited his horizon. "I am going into the Army first," he said, "but I mean to have a public career." He had been badly disturbed by his Harrow record. "I had achieved no distinction. It is not pleasant to feel oneself so hopelessly outclassed and left behind at the very beginning of the race."

It took him three tries and much cramming with a private tutor before he was admitted to Sandhurst, the British equivalent of the American West Point. He was now a gentleman cadet. His American grandfather had once said this about gentlemen: "The character of a gentleman I consider within the capacity of all—at least it requires no extraordinary intellect." But Winston's father thought differently.

Lord Randolph had resigned as Chancellor of the Exchequer on an issue of budget economy, and resigned his position as Leader of the House of Commons. He was thirty-seven years old then, and his wife privately lamented, "He has thrown himself from the top of the ladder and will never reach it again." She refused to return her husband's robes as Chancellor, said she was putting them in an old tin box, saving them for her son.

But her son now wanted the soldier's life. After he had barely scraped into Sandhurst, Winston received a long, severe letter from his father, predicting a bleak future, warning of the danger of his becoming "a social wastrel." His father even wrote a letter to a friend in South Africa, asking whether he could find a place there for his son, because he did not believe his son could make a career in England.

"Only once did he lift his visor in my sight," said Winston of his father. It was in the autumn of 1892 at their house in Newmarket. Young Winston had fired a double-barreled shotgun at a rabbit on the lawn and an angry father reported his son for disturbing him. Seeing his son distressed, the father quickly changed his tone. "I then had one of the three or four long intimate conversations with him which are all I can boast.

"He proceeded to talk to me in the most wonderful and captivating manner about school and going into the Army and the grown-up life which lay beyond. I listened spellbound to this sudden complete departure from his usual reserve, amazed at his intimate comprehension of all my affairs."

BELOW. Winston was graduated from Sandhurst with honors in 1894, eighth in a class of 150, was commissioned a second lieutenant in the Fourth Hussars at Aldershot. It was an era of unbroken peace and scarce adventure, and Churchill's young men felt that their chance for medals and bravery might never come again. "The young soldier who had been 'on active service' and 'under fire' had an aura about him to which the generals he served under, the troopers he led, and the girls he courted, accorded a unanimous, sincere and spontaneous recognition," wrote Churchill.

But polo might count for something, he admitted.

Polo taught discipline and comradeship, the satisfaction of intricate, loyal teamwork, plus the pleasure of hitting the ball.

Winston spent most of his money buying horses, later leveled this advice to wealthy parents: "Don't give your son money . . . give him horses. Young men have often been ruined through owning horses or through backing horses, but never through riding them; unless, of course, they break their necks, which, taken at a gallop, is a very good death to die."

"I think I was pretty well trained to sit and manage a horse," he said. "This is one of the most important things in the world." He then described the thrill of a glittering jingle of a cavalry squadron maneuvering at the trot, the excitement when they go into a gallop, the stir of the horses, the clank of equipment, the thrill of motion, the tossing plumes, the dignity of the uniform, the sense of incorporation in a living machine.

He was twenty-two in 1896, no longer pompous about reading. At school, when they had handed him Aristotle's *Ethics,* his only comment was, "It is extraordinary how much of this I had already thought out for myself." Now he suddenly realized he had only "the vaguest knowledge about many large spheres of thought." He therefore wrote his mother asking for books on history, philosophy, economics. She immediately sent him eight volumes of Gibbon's *Decline and Fall of the Roman Empire,* and it influenced the sense and style of her son as much as it had influenced her husband's.

After filling his mind, he now wanted to fill his spirit, his need for adventure. Because the only war going on was in Cuba, Winston and a friend went together and he heard the first whistle of close bullets, one of which killed a horse directly behind him (and he also picked up the siesta habit, which proved useful in another war).

Later, Churchill said, "When young men begged to be allowed to take part in actual fighting and when the curmudgeons of red tape interposed their veto, I used to brush these objections aside, saying, 'After all, they were only asking to stop a bullet. Let them have their way.' "

> So today—and oh! if ever
> Duty's voice is ringing clear
> Bidding men to brave endeavor—
> Be our answer, "We are here."

This had been one of Churchill's favorite verses of one of his favorite songs at Harrow, and it was part of his life.

The Afridi tribes were fighting British soldiers in India's Mamund Valley and Churchill hurried there to rejoin his Fourth Hussars. Second Lieutenant Churchill could communicate with his native soldiers with only three words: 'Maro' (kill), 'chalo' (get on), and 'Tally Ho,' which, he said, "speaks for itself." His native troops watched him carefully. When he grinned, they grinned—so he grinned often. In between grins, he described the campaign for the London *Daily Telegraph* and the *Pioneer* (a war-correspondent assignment his mother had helped arrange) for five pounds a column.

He wrote:

"A shrill crying rose from many points. Yi! Yi! Yi! Bang! Bang! Bang! The whole hillside began to be spotted with smoke, and tiny figures descended every moment nearer towards us. Our eight Sikhs opened an independent fire, which soon became more and more rapid. The hostile figures continued to flow down the mountainside and scores began to gather in rocks about a hundred yards away from us. The targets were too tempting to be resisted. I borrowed the Martini of the Sikh by whom I lay. I began to shoot carefully at the men gathering in the rocks. A lot of bullets whistled around us . . .

"... Out from the edge of houses rushed a half-dozen Pathan swordsmen. The bearers of a poor wounded adjutant let him fall and fled at their approach. The leading tribesman rushed upon the prostrate figure and slashed it three or four times with his sword. I forgot everything else at this moment except a desire to kill this man. I wore my long cavalry sword well sharpened. After all, I had won the Public School fencing medal. I resolved on personal combat *à l'arme blanche.* The savage saw me coming. I was not more than twenty yards away. He picked up a big stone and hurled it at me with his left hand, and then awaited me, brandishing his sword. There were others waiting not far behind him. . . ."

Then came a fusillade of bullets and he raced for a knoll.

"... One man was shot through the breast and pouring with blood; another lay on his back kicking and twisting. The British officer was spinning around just behind me, his face a mass of blood, his right eye cut out.

"Yes, it was certainly an adventure."

BELOW. Churchill wrote a book about it, *The Malakland Field Force,* in which he wrote critically of his superiors. Word came of this to Commander in Chief Sir Herbert Kitchener (seated, center), now transferred to another hot spot, the Sudan. So, when soldier-correspondent Winston Churchill tried to switch to the Sudan, he found Kitchener an immovable obstacle.

Churchill afterwards referred to "General Kitchener, who never spares himself, cares little for others. He treated all men like machines."

Critics called Churchill a self-advertiser and a medal-hunter, but he kept maneuvering for transfer. When

the Governor General of Bombay, Lord Sandhurst, asked him questions, "I thought it would be unbecoming for me not to reply fully. There were indeed moments when he seemed willing to impart his own views; but I thought it would be ungracious to put him to so much trouble; and he very readily subsided."

His mother was much more diplomatic, pulled all her silken strings, and Churchill finally received this War Office telegram:

You have been attached as a supernumerary lieutenant to the 21st Lancers for the Soudan campaign. You are to report at once to the Abassiyeh Barracks, Cairo, to the regimental headquarters. It is understood you will proceed at your own expense and that in the event of your being killed or wounded in the impending operations, or for any other reason, no charge of any kind will fall on British Army funds.

The president of the Psychical Research Society dined with Churchill soon after he had received the telegram, and extracted a promise from Churchill that if anything "unfortunate" should happen to him, and he was killed, he would promptly "communicate" with him.

More practically, Churchill arranged with the *Morning Post* to serve as their war correspondent, this time for fifteen pounds a column.

Kitchener prepared for his coming, put him in charge of a decrepit mule and two donkeys.

ABOVE. "This is an hour to live," he wrote, after being given command of a troop of lancers, better known as "the saucy devils." "They are advancing and advancing fast," he wrote. "A tide is coming in. . . . The trumpet sounded 'Right wheel in line' and all the sixteen troops swung towards the blue-black riflemen. Almost immediately the regiment broke into a gallop, and the 21st Lancers were committed to their first charge of the war.

"Not ten yards away, two blue men lay in my path. They were perhaps a couple yards apart. I rode at the interval between them. They both fired. I passed through the smoke conscious that I was unhurt. The trooper immediately behind me was killed at this place and at this moment, whether by these shots or not I do not know.

". . . Life is a whole and luck is a whole, and no part of them can be separated from the rest." BELOW. "Nothing like the Battle of Omdurman will ever be seen again," he wrote. "It was the last link in the long chain of those spectacular conflicts whose vivid and majestic splendor has done so much to invest war with glamor. Everything was visible to the naked eyes. The armies marched and maneuvered in the crisp surface of the desert plain through which the Nile wandered . . .

"As I straightened myself in the saddle, I saw before me another figure with an uplifted sword. I raised my pistol and fired. So close were we that the pistol itself actually struck him. Man and sword disappeared below and behind me . . .

"I looked back at the Dervish mass. I saw two or three riflemen crouching and aiming their rifles at me from the fringe of it. Then for the first time that morning, I experienced a sudden sensation of fear. I thought these riflemen would hit me and the rest devour me like wolves."

He spurred his horse and drew clear of the melee. Then he saw the apparitions of war: ". . . horses spouting blood, struggling on three legs, men staggering on foot, men bleeding from terrible wounds, fishhook spears stuck right through them, arms and faces cut to pieces, bowels protruding, men gasping, crying, collapsing, expiring . . ."

Back at Harrow, a redheaded little boy had had his own battle cry to spur him on at such times: "St. George, St. Dunstan and the Devil. . . ."

LEFT. Back in London, there was an election in Oldham and the Conservative party persuaded Churchill to run for a seat in the House of Commons. It was 1899 and he was twenty-three years old. He lost by 1,800 votes and the recriminations came fast. "I thought he was a young man of promise," said one critic, "but it appears he is a young man of promises."

"Everyone threw the blame on me," said Churchill. "I have noticed that they nearly always do. I suppose it is because they think I shall be able to bear it best."

But Conservative party leader Balfour wrote him a note: "Never mind, it will all come right; and this small reverse will have no permanent ill effect upon your political fortunes."

Earlier, he had had a greater loss: the woman he knew best and the man he knew least—his nurse and his father. Mrs. Everest was seriously ill when he rushed to see her.

"She knew she was in danger," said Churchill, "but her only anxiety was for me. There had been a heavy shower of rain. My jacket was wet. When she felt it with her hands, she was greatly alarmed for fear I should catch cold."

"She had been my dearest and most intimate friend," he said.

His father died at the age of forty-six, a beaten, broken man. "All my dreams of comradeship with him, of entering Parliament at his side and in his support, were ended," Churchill wrote. "There remained for me only to pursue his aims and vindicate his memory." RIGHT. The turn of the century was only a few months away when the Boer War broke out. His nerves braced, his imagination stirred, Winston Churchill was ready.

ABOVE. He had written another book, *The River War,* for which his mother again acted as agent, arranging publication. The book had a huge popular success, even winning the praise of the Prince of Wales, soon to be King Edward VII. The *Morning Post* hired him as its principal war correspondent, and his mother again helped manage a simultaneous military commission, first lieutenant in the South African Light Horse, a regiment of six squadrons and seven hundred mounted men, with a battery of galloping Colt machines. BELOW. Despite their previous unkind cuts towards each other, Lord Kitchener (seated center) and Churchill (second from left, standing) learned a more mutual respect. Churchill had bicycled through Johannesburg in civilian clothes, while the city was still in Boer hands, and reported his military observations to Kitchener.

Churchill counted the two months fighting for the relief of Ladysmith as one of his happiest memories.

It was a war of the occasional skirmish, casualties from a half dozen to a score.

"I saw all there was to see," he wrote. "Day after day we rode out in the early morning on one flank or another and played about with the Boers, galloped around or clambered up the rocky hills, caught glimpses of darting fleeing horsemen in the distance, heard a few bullets whistle, had a few careful shots and came safe home to a good dinner and cheery keenly-intelligent companions.

"We lived in great comfort in the open air, with cool nights and bright sunshine, with plenty of meat, chickens and beer. The excellent Natal newspapers often got into the firing line about noon and always awaited us on our return in the evening. Carefree, no regrets for the past, no fears for the future: no expense, no duns, no complications and all the time my salary was safely piling up at home."

He remembered an occasional discomfort in the field, sharing a blanket with a Colonel Byng on a chilly night. "When he turned over, I was in the cold. When I turned over, I pulled the blanket off him and he objected. He was the Colonel. It was not a good arrangement."

Another time, in a skirmish, his terrified horse plunged and threw him in an open field, but Churchill, doubled up on another's horse that had been hard hit, still managed to get away.

"This kind of war was full of fascinating thrills," said Churchill. "Nobody expected to be killed . . . a sporting element in a splendid game."

Meanwhile his American mother had captivated an American millionaire, persuaded him to buy, equip and staff a floating hospital ship and sailed it to South Africa to pick up wounded. One of her first casualties was her son Jack (above), and her son Winston arrived soon afterwards for a short visit. In a series of letters which she published in the *Anglo-Saxon Review* (of which she was editor), she wrote, "It was hard to say goodbye to the two boys."

His mother also persuaded a general to permit her a tour of the front, had a 4.7 gun named after her, managed to catch up again with son Winston near Ladysmith, ". . . and we could see and understand everything with the help of Winston's graphic tongue." Before she left, she wrote, "I longed to be a man to take some part in the fighting." And when she saw an armored-car disaster, she wrote, "I thanked God my son Winston was not there."

ABOVE. But son Winston had been in another disaster, an armored train carrying two companies of infantry, ambushed by Boers at Estcourt. Churchill helped load the wounded from some of the six derailed coaches onto an engine car, and got it going, while he and others stayed behind to provide covering fire. "Keep cool, men," he told them. "This will be interesting for my paper."

But Churchill soon found himself staring into a rifle held by a mounted Boer. Taken prisoner, he was marched sixty miles to a train, then onto a prisoner-of-war camp in Pretoria. "We are not going to let you go, old chappie, although you are a correspondent. We don't catch the son of a lord every day."

Years later, a Boer general visited England to discuss a loan, and was introduced to Churchill as General Botha, soon to be the first Prime Minister of Transvaal. In their talk, Churchill told Botha of his Boer experience, and Botha, smiling, said, "Don't you recognize me? I was that man. It was I who took you prisoner. I, myself."

BELOW. "Prisoner of war!" Churchill wrote afterwards, "You are in the power of your enemy. You owe your life to his humanity, and your daily bread to his compassion. You must obey his orders, go where he tells you to go, stay where he tells you, await his pleasure, possess your soul in patience. Meanwhile the war is going on, great events are in progress, fine opportunities for action and adventure are slipping away . . .

£25.—.—

(vijf en twintig pond stg.)
belooning uitgeloofd door
de Sub.Commissie van Wijk V
voor den Specialen Constabel
dezer wijk, die den ontvluchte
Krijgsgevangene
Churchill
levend of dood te dezer kantore
aflevert.

Namens de Sub-Comm.
wijk V

Translation.

£25

(Twenty-five Pounds stg.) REWARD is offered by the
Sub-Commission of the fifth division, on behalf of the Special Constable
of the said division, to anyone who brings the escaped prisoner of war

CHURCHILL,

dead or alive to this office.

For the Sub-Commission of the fifth division.
(Signed) LODK. de HAAS, Sec.

NOTE.- The Original Reward for the arrest of Winston Churchill on his escape from Pretoria, posted on the Government Doors of
Pretoria, brought to England by the Hon. Harry Hanham, and is now the property of W. R. Barton.

"I certainly hated every minute of my captivity more than I have ever hated any other period in my whole life."
ABOVE. He decided to escape.

"Now or never! I stood on a ledge, seized the top of the wall with my hands, and drew myself up. Twice I let myself down again in sickly hesitation, and then with a third resolve scrambled up and over.

"I was free!"

BELOW. A description added: "Englishman about twenty-five years old, about five feet eight inches tall, indifferent build, walks with a forward stoop, pale appearance, red-brownish hair, small and hardly noticeable mustache, talks through his nose and cannot pronounce the letter 'S' properly."

ABOVE. "I reached Durban to find myself a popular hero," Churchill wrote. "I was received as if I had won a great victory. The harbor was decorated with flags. Bands and crowd thronged the quays." BELOW. "The Admiral, the General, the Mayor pressed on board to grasp my hand. I was nearly torn to pieces by enthusiastic kindness."

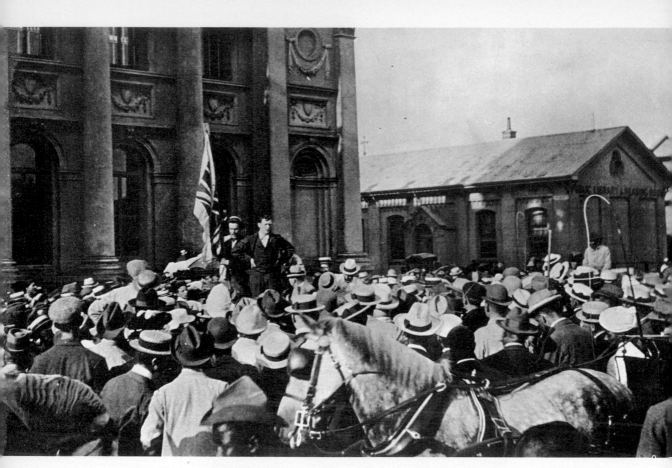

"Whirled along the shoulders of the crowd, I was carried to the steps of the Town Hall, where nothing would content them but a speech, which, after a becoming reluctance, I was induced to deliver. Sheaves of telegrams from all parts of the world poured in upon me, and I started that night for the Army in a blaze of triumph."

HOW I ESCAPED
FROM PRETORIA.

By Winston Churchill.

THE *Morning Post* has received the following telegram from Mr. Winston Spencer Churchill, its war correspondent, who was taken prisoner by the Boers and escaped from Pretoria.

LOURENCO MARQUES, December 21st, 10 p.m.

I was concealed in a railway truck under great sacks.

I had a small store of good water with me.

I remained hidden, chancing discovery.

The Boers searched the train at Komati Poort, but did not search deep enough, so after sixty hours of misery I came safely here.

I am very weak, but I am free.

I have lost many pounds weight, but I am lighter in heart.

I shall also avail myself of every opportunity from this moment to urge with earnestness an unflinching and uncompromising prosecution of the war.

On the afternoon of the 12th the Transvaal Government's Secretary for War informed me that there was little chance of my release.

I therefore resolved to escape the same night, and left the State Schools Prison at Pretoria by climbing the wall when the sentries' backs were turned momentarily.

I walked through the streets of the town without any disguise, meeting many burghers, but I was not challenged in the crowd.

I got through the pickets of the Town Guard, and struck the Delagoa Bay Railroad.

I walked along it, evading the watchers at the bridges and culverts.

I waited for a train beyond the first station.

The out 11.10 goods train from Pretoria arrived, and before it had reached full speed I boarded with great difficulty, and hid myself under coal sacks.

I jumped from the train before dawn, and sheltered during the day in a small wood, in company with a huge vulture, who displayed a lively interest in me.

I walked on at dusk.

There were no more trains that night.

The danger of meeting the guards of the railway line continued; but I was obliged to follow it, as I had no compass or map.

I had to make wide *détours* to avoid the bridges, stations, and huts.

My progress was very slow, and chocolate is not a satisfying food.

The outlook was gloomy, but I persevered, with God's help, for five days.

The food I had to have was very precarious.

I was lying up at daylight, and walking on at night time, and, meanwhile, my escape had been discovered and my description telegraphed everywhere.

All the trains were searched.

Everyone was on the watch for me.

Four wrong people were arrested.

But on the sixth day I managed to board a train beyond Middleburg, whence there is a direct service to Delagoa.

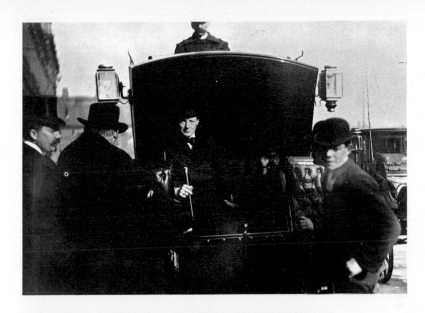

ABOVE. His popularity reached such a peak that somebody even wrote a song about him:

> You've heard of Winston Churchill—
> That's all I need to say.
> He's the latest and the greatest
> Correspondent of his day.

Churchill's first condition for success was to get enough money to live on without asking anybody for anything. He signed up for a series of lectures throughout the United States, was surprised to find them not much excited about the Boer War. He found American audiences cool and critical, but also good-natured, urbane, friendly. BELOW. Mark Twain (shown here greeting King Edward VII and Queen Alexandra) also served as host at Churchill's first lecture, and introduced him by saying, "By his father, he is an Englishman; by his mother, an American. Behold, the perfect man!"

Churchill, who had read most of Twain's books, and deeply admired him, received a fresh set of thirty Twain volumes, with the inscription, "To do good is noble, to teach others to do good is nobler, and no trouble."

61

He took time out to make a bet on the British Empire . . .

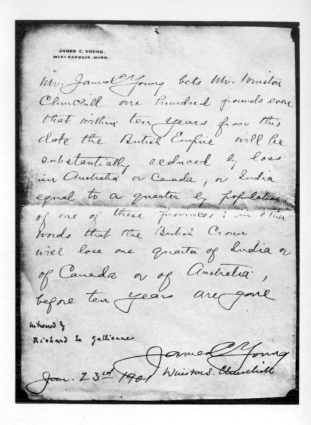

. . . and meet an American novelist, also named Winston Churchill, whom he also admired—except that he had received some of his letters and bills by mistake. In his note, the British Churchill wrote, "Mr. Winston Churchill presents his compliments to Mr. Winston Churchill, and begs to draw his attention to a matter which concerns them both."

ABOVE. Back in England, they called 1900 "the khaki election," because so many soldiers were running. One of them was Winston Churchill, this time determined to win. But the suffragettes, who had fought him hard the previous year, fought him again. They grabbed and yanked him, threw coke at him, and one suffragette even struck him three times with her riding whip during his speech at Bristol. "Now you will understand we must have our vote," she said.   BELOW. Without committing himself to them, all Churchill said was, "Trust in me, ladies."

ABOVE. When a feminist asked Churchill his view on the role of women in the future, he answered, "The same, I trust, as it has been since the days of Adam and Eve." And when some suffragettes chained themselves to a railing, swearing to stay there until they got the vote, Churchill commented, "A man might as well chain himself to the railings of St. Thomas Hospital and say he would not move until he had a baby." BELOW. Then, and later, his mother campaigned with him. "We worked together like brother and sister," said Churchill. Richard Harding Davis, another famous war correspondent, wrote: "Winston Churchill was always so precocious I cannot recall the time when he was young enough to be Lady Randolph's son. Certainly I cannot recall the time when she was old enough to be his mother."

Widowed at forty, she centered much of her social energy to further the future of her son. When Queen Victoria pinned the Order of the Crown of India on Mrs. Churchill (and stuck her), she was near the summit of British society.

ABOVE. Women or no women, he won the election . . . BELOW. . . . and became the Conservative Member in the House of Commons from Oldham. When they introduced him to make his maiden speech in the House, ". . . the butter was laid on with a trowel. . . . When he descanted upon my 'bravery with a sword and brilliancy with the pen' I feared the audience would cry out 'Oh rats!' "

His speech asked for fairness to the Boers, and he was pleased that the audience cheered at all the right places ". . . when I paused on purpose to give them a chance, and even at others which I had not foreseen. At the end they clapped loudly and for quite a long time.

"I could do it after all."

After the speech, he thanked the House for having listened to him, "Not for anything I have to say but for the memory of one who once, for a brief period, led this House."

ABOVE. The father and son had the same large eyes and square forehead, the same habit of throwing back their heads and laughing loudly at anything that amused them and the same mannerisms—even their voices, resonant with a touch of asperity, were curiously similar. BELOW. "Winston even copied his father in his little tricks of manner," wrote Richard Harding Davis. "Standing with hands shoved under the frock coat and one resting on each hip as though squeezing in the waistline; when seated, resting the elbows on the arms of the chair and nervously locking and unclasping fingers, are tricks common to both."

ABOVE. He left the Conservative party in 1904 on the issue of free trade. He switched to the Liberal party, saying that he wanted ". . . a government that will think a little more about the toiler at the bottom of the mine and a little less about the fluctuations of the share market in London." The Liberals swept into office the next year and Churchill got his first government job, "Under-Secretary of State for the Colonies," and promptly took a trip to Africa. BELOW. . . . took a ride on a cowcatcher . . .

. . . climbed an observation ladder at a hippopotamus camp . . .

. . . and killed a rare white rhinoceros.

ABOVE. "If you are young," he once said, "get married and have babies."   BELOW. "Where does a family start?" he said. "It starts with a young man falling in love with a girl—no superior alternative has yet been found."

ABOVE. Long before he got out of this cab at Caxton Hall to get his marriage license, his maternal grandmother, Clara Jerome, had been a close friend of Lady Blanche Hosier and her mother, the Countess of Airlie. Lady Hosier's husband, Col. Sir Henry Hosier, had died in China, where he had served with the Third Dragoons. He left a daughter, Clementine.

It was at a ball given by her grandmother, the Countess, in the spring of 1908, that Clementine met Winston. The last time they had met didn't really count—it was at a children's party; he was at Harrow and she was only five.

"I remember," said Clementine's friend, "that she wore a satin white princess dress which suited her wonderfully."

It suited Winston even more.   BELOW. "My marriage was much the most fortunate and joyous event which happened to me in the whole of my life," said Winston, "for what can be more glorious than to be united in one's walk through life with a being incapable of an ignoble thought."

He later wrote, "We were married on Sept. 12, 1908—and lived happily ever afterwards."

70

ABOVE. He called her "Dear Cat." BELOW. She called him "Dear Pig."

The wedding account mentions that, ". . . the list of wedding presents fills two columns of small type." The presents included a few duplicates: twenty-five candlesticks, twenty-one inkstands, twenty silver bowls, fifteen vases, fourteen silver trays, eight sets of salt cellars and ten cigarette cases.

The bride wore a lovely veil of point de Venise lace which Lady Randolph had worn at her own wedding.

They honeymooned the first few days at Blenheim Palace, then headed for France, where they saw friends (Duchess of Sutherland, below) went on to Italy and then returned to London, renting their first house at Queen Anne's Gate. Churchill was then president of the Board of Trade. He was thirty-three.

"If you want to know about elections," he once wrote, "I am the man to tell you." At various times, he was a candidate in Oldham, Northwest Manchester, Dundee, West Leicester, the Abbey Division of Westminster, the Epping Division of Essex and the Woodford Division. He ran thirteen times, lost five. Of all things, he considered the election speech the most vital:

". . . In those days and indeed for many years," he wrote, "I was unable to say anything (except a sentence in rejoinder) that I had not written out and committed to memory beforehand. I had never had the practice which comes to young men at the University of speaking in small debating societies impromptu upon all sorts of subjects.

"The general verdict was not unfavorable. Although many guessed I had learnt it by heart, this was pardoned because of the pains I had taken."

Churchill wrote a novel called *Savrola,* set in a mythical Mediterranean republic, in which his hero has many of the Churchill qualities. In it, he says of this hero:

"His speech—he had made many and knew that nothing good can be obtained without effort. These impromptu feats of oratory existed only in the mind of the listeners; the flowers of rhetoric were hothouse plants.

"His ideas began to take the form of words, to group themselves into sentences; he murmured to himself; the rhythm of his own language swayed him; instinctively he alliterated. Ideas succeeded one another, as a stream flows swiftly by and the light changes on its waters.

"What a game it was! His brain contained the cards he had to play, the world the stakes he played for."

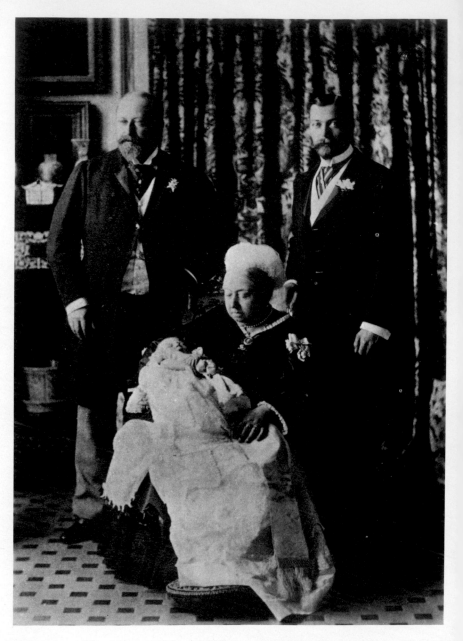

Queen Victoria died in 1901, ending an era. Her own son Edward VII (standing, left) lived as king until 1910. Then his son George V (standing, right) became king. Queen Victoria holds another king in her lap, the future Edward VIII. Winston Churchill served them all—and two more, George VI and Queen Elizabeth.

The King is dead . . .

. . . long live . . .

. . . the King.

ABOVE. Home Secretary Winston Churchill was in his bath when an aide rushed in to say that two anarchists had killed a policeman and were barricaded in a building and the police wanted to know if he would call out the troops. Churchill promptly rushed down to Sidney Street to take command. BELOW. Churchill quickly set up battle headquarters and sent frequent reports to the press.

"The Battle of Stepney"
Mr. Winston Churchill surrounded by Detectives and Armed Police

ABOVE. He later said that his ". . . conviction of duty was supported by a strong sense of curiosity." BELOW. British novelist H. G. Wells had once said of Churchill, "There are times when . . . I can think of him only as an intractable little boy, a mischievous little boy, a knee-worthy little boy. Only by thinking of him in that way can I go on liking him."

At an inquest into the whole affair, the Churchill critics said they could understand what the press photographers were doing, but not what the Home Secretary was doing, getting himself photographed standing in an East End doorway under fire. While Churchill tried to explain, his brother Jack (hand on chin) listened.

About this time, there had been a threat of kidnaping of Churchill's first child, his son Randolph, and the nurse had a detective escort.

The Home Secretary had many uniforms . . .

... and many duties.

He and his wife played golf . . .

. . . and rode together.

He loved to shoot and hunt . . .

. . . but, best of all, loved to play polo.

"To get at Churchill's angle in life," said Patrick Thompson, "you want to see him play polo. He rides in the game like heavy cavalry getting into position for the assault. He trots about, keenly watchful, biding his time, a master of tactics and strategy. Abruptly he sees his chance, and he gathers his pony and charges in, neither deft nor graceful, but full of tearing physical energy—and skillful with it too.

"He bears down opposition by the weight of his dash, and strikes the ball. Did I say 'strikes'? It is the wrong word. He slashes the ball."

Churchill played polo until he was fifty.

Meanwhile he was willing to try other contraptions . . .

. . . some of which, he thought, had a military potential.

Churchill felt the threat of war, visited German maneuvers at Silesia, shook hands with Kaiser Wilhelm II . . .

ABOVE. . . . but the handshaking days were soon over. German troops intensified their training.   BELOW. Even th
schoolboys at Prussian schools took on a more military tone.

He now served King George V as First Lord of the Admiralty.

ABOVE. While the British Tommies trained with bayonets . . . BELOW. . . . the boys at Eton practiced with their rif

92

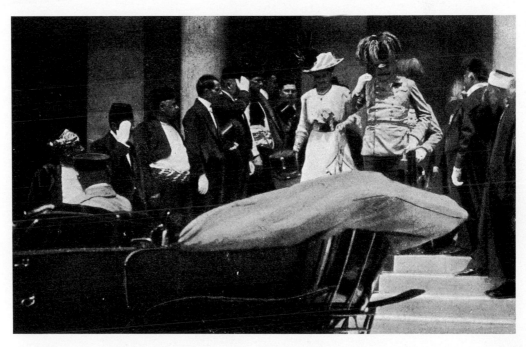

And then, one day in 1914 in Sarajevo . . .

"All the News That's
Fit to Print."

THE WEATHER

NEW YORK, MONDAY, JUNE 29, 1914.—EIGHTEEN PAGES.

ONE CENT

GUERRA!

HEIR TO AUSTRIA'S THRONE IS SLAIN WITH HIS WIFE BY A BOSNIAN YOUTH TO AVENGE SEIZURE OF HIS COUNTRY

**Francis Ferdinand Shot
During State Visit
to Sarajevo.**

TWO ATTACKS IN A DAY

Archduke Saves His Life First
Time by Knocking Aside a
Bomb Hurled at Auto.

SLAIN IN SECOND ATTEMPT

Lad Dashes at Car as the Royal
Couple Return from Town Hall
and Kills Both of Them.

LAID TO A SERVIAN PLOT

Heir Warned Not to Go to Bos-
nia, Where Populace Met
Him with Servian Flags.

Archduke Francis Ferdinand and his Consort the Duchess of Hohenberg

Slain by Assassin's Bullets.

. . . a young Austrian prince was murdered.

The game of Army maneuvers . . .

. . . became the grimness of war.

95

It was Lord Kitchener, a one-time caustic critic of a young subaltern, who came to Churchill on the eve of war and said to the First Lord of the Admiralty, "Well, there is one thing at any rate they cannot take from you—the fleet is ready."

The boy who had once plotted intricate battles with his toy soldiers, the young lieutenant who had seen more real war than half the generals of Europe had, now became the young statesman calling at 10 Downing Street, again offering his services to king and country.

MEN OF LONDON

NOW IS THE TIME

"The British Empire is fighting for its existence."
Lord Kitchener.

Nearest Recruiting Office:

Holborn Hall.

"I shall want more men and still more until the enemy is crushed."
Lord Kitchener.

Come forward now and be trained to do your share.

Every fit man owes this duty to himself and to his country.

"It's a Long Way to Tipperary . . ."

"I Didn't Raise My Boy to Be a Soldier . . ."

The great concern of the Admiralty . . .

. . . was German submarine warfare.

And then a new kind of warfare . . .

". . . The Zeppelins are coming . . ."

Churchill introduced an Air arm into the Navy.

102

Few saw its future as sharply as he did.

103

Publicly, the Churchill image became the image of energetic preparedness; privately, some critics complained that "Winston is too big for his boots." His pet project was to invade the "soft under-belly" of the Dardanelles, knock out Turkey and supply Russia. His naval chief, Lord Fisher, told him, "You are bent on forcing the Dardanelles and nothing will turn you from it—*nothing*. I know you so well." Fisher resigned; Churchill went ahead.

ABOVE. The Dardanelles proved a fiasco, costly in lives, and the British evacuated Gallipoli, the full blame falling on Churchill. "Everything I got, I have fought for," he said. "And yet I have been hated more than anybody."

But Churchill felt crushed, resigned his office and told a friend, "I am finished."

ABOVE. At the later inquiry, he told them, "Your commission may condemn the men who tried to force the Dardanelles, but your children will keep their condemnation for all who did not rally to their aid." Afterwards, he commented, "Searching my heart, I cannot regret the effort. It was good to go as far as we did. Not to persevere —that was the crime." About something else, years later, he said, "Perhaps it is better to be irresponsible and right than responsible and wrong."

Churchill was put in charge of the 6th Royal Scots Fusiliers. Writing of Churchill's day-and-night inspections of the trenches, an adjutant wrote of an enemy bombardment, "At that moment, I profoundly hated war, but at that and every moment, I believe, Winston Churchill reveled in it. There was no such thing as fear in him."

Churchill himself put it another way. "I must go to the front," he said. "I hate being cold. I loathe being ordered about. But the Tommies will understand. The wounded boys always give me a cheer. They'll see what I mean."

He decided that soldiering was simpler than statesmanship.

ABOVE. The two men of Europe who saw and pushed the future of the tank were Charles de Gaulle of France and Winston Churchill of Britain. Back in 1914, Churchill asked Admiral Bacon to produce a design of a caterpillar tractor that would cross trenches, then ordered eighteen of these "land ships" on his own responsibility at an estimated cost of seventy thousand pounds. BELOW. "War, which used to be cruel and magnificent, has now become cruel and squalid," he said. "Instead of a small number of well-trained professionals championing their country's cause with ancient weapons and a beautiful intricacy of armchair maneuver, sustained at every moment by the applause of their nation, we now have entire populations, including even women and children, pitted against one another in brutish mutual extermination, and only a set of bleary-eyed clerks left to add up the butcher's bill. . . .

"To hell with it!"

With David Lloyd George elected as Prime Minister, Churchill was called back to become Minister of Munitions.

ABOVE. He found twelve thousand officials in fifty departments, each of whom claimed direct access to himself, and he also discovered a shortage of artillery shells for the front. He changed both situations. And he toured the factories, buoying up morale . . . BELOW. . . . and he made some converts.

ABOVE. Transferred to the job as Secretary of State for War, Churchill handled the touchy demobilization problem. In the left foreground is Lt. Col. Bernard Montgomery, who became the Field Marshal of British Armies in a future war. It was Montgomery who said to Churchill, "I don't drink and I don't smoke and I am one hundred percent fit." Churchill answered, "I drink and I smoke and I am two hundred percent fit." BELOW. With the war's end, Churchill rode in the Victory Parade with General Pershing, who had headed the American Expeditionary Forces.

The British Tommies marched in victory . . .

The Germans straggled in their defeat

Politics was always with him—and so was his wife. During the war, she had been in charge of feeding some three hundred thousand people a week.

She went with him to meetings . . .

With their son, Randolph, she answered his mail and took messages.

ABOVE. She held his umbrella—and his hand.   BELOW. She even made speeches for him. At meetings he attended, the crowd usually gave him three cheers at the end, and he always asked for another one for his wife—and it was usually the loudest cheer of all.

Churchill insisted on a summarized report of polling progress taken at two-hour intervals, and at the end of each day's work carefully studied a full account of the canvassing, then passed on fresh instructions to his election agent. But sometimes he still lost. When he lost in the Dundee election in 1922, he was hospitalized for an operation on his appendix and he quipped afterwards, "I am without an office, without a seat and without an appendix."

But what possibly made the hurt worse was that he was defeated by a Prohibitionist, a Mr. Scrymgeour.

Years before, he had said, "My father is Chancellor of the Exchequer and that's what I'm going to be, too." Meanwhile, he had also been Secretary of State for War and Air (he had kept a strict record of the mileage on his air-force car for any private business, and paid for what gas he used), and Colonial Secretary, in which office he had played a key role in setting up the Irish Free State. ("Tell Winston we could never have done anything without him," said nationalist Michael Collins. Previously Collins had complained to Churchill, "You hunted me night and day! You put a price on my head!" And Churchill had said, "Wait a minute; you are not the only one." And Churchill took from his wall the framed copy of the reward offered by the Boers for his recapture. "At any rate, yours was a good price," said Churchill to Collins. "Five thousand pounds. Look at mine—twenty-five pounds, dead or alive. How do you like that?" Collins read it, laughed hard and all irritation vanished.)

And now he was Chancellor of the Exchequer, wearing his father's robes that his mother had saved in an old tin box, but never lived long enough to see her son wear.

He took the Exchequer job in 1924, held it for five years but probably liked it least of all his government jobs. He was so much more interested in facts than he was in figures that he could never work himself up to any proper pitch of excitement about making a four-hour speech on a de-rating plan for industry.

But, for him, there was an interval of fun, almost glee. There was the British general strike in 1926, shutting everything down, including the newspapers. Churchill decided that the public had a right to know what was going on, and so he became editor and publisher of a newspaper he called the *British Gazette*. He said, "I decline utterly to be impartial as between the fire brigade and the fire."

The Briti

Published by His

GENERAL STRIKE OFF

THE

UNCONDITIONAL WITHDRAWAL OF NOTICES BY T.U.C.

Men To Return Forthwith.

SURRENDER RECEIVED BY PREMIER IN DOWNING STREET.

Negotiations To Be Resumed In The Coal Dispute.

The General Strike, which began at midnight on Monday, May 3, ended yesterday in an unconditional withdrawal of the strike notices by the General Council of the Trades Union Congress. The news of the settlement was conveyed to the public in the following official communiqué :—

WHITEHALL, May 12.

It was intimated to the Prime Minister that the Trades Union Council desired to come and see him at Downing-street, and they arrived soon after 12 noon. Mr. Pugh made a statement, in which he stated that the Trades Union Council had decided to call off the strike notices forthwith.

The Prime Minister then spoke briefly. He stated that he was very glad to hear what Mr. Pugh had said, and he would report it to his colleagues in the Cabinet.

As regards the coal industry, the Prime Minister said that negotiations would be resumed, and the Government would consider as to what steps should be taken.

The whole proceedings lasted a very few minutes.

NO RESUMPTION BY MINERS.

Mr. Cook And End Of The General Strike.

"Nothing To Do With Us."

Following upon a meeting of the Miners' Federation Committee yesterday morning the following telegram was sent to all the coal-fields :—

"Miners must not resume work pending the decision of the National Conference convened for Friday next at the Kingsway Hall, London, 10 a.m. Please send delegates.—Cook, Secretary."

The Miners' Executive sat in conference for the greater part of the afternoon and eventually adjourned until ten o'clock this morning. After the adjournment Mr. A. J. Cook made the following official statement, explaining that it was the Miners' reply to the proposals put before them by the T.U.C. on Tuesday night :—

"In view of the statement made in the T.U.C. draft received after they had met Sir Herbert Samuel, the miners discussed the same and passed the following resolution :—

"'That the Miners' Executive have given grave and patient consideration to the draft proposals prepared by the T.U.C. Negotiating Committee and endorsed by the General Council representing what they call the best terms which can be obtained to settle the present crisis in the coal industry. The Miners' Executive regret the fact that no opportunity for consideration was afforded the accredited representatives of the Miners' Federation on the Negotiating Committee in the preparation of the draft or in the discussions of May 11 leading thereto.

"'At the best the proposals imply a reduction of the wage rates for a large number of mine workers, which is contrary to the repeated declarations of

THE K

Appea

DIFF

"Let Us

The Ki following ham Palac

TC

The N through a It was to General S an end.

At such important people to situation task requ able and country. will be d impossible

Let us of bittern few days remember orderly t though s with add of bringir will be l the past, with the

Gazette

ty's Stationery Office.

MAY 13, 1926.   ONE PENNY.

O THE

Lasting

STILL

ements of

issued the
Bucking-

LE.

ust passed
me anxiety.
d that the
brought to

supremely
ther all my
e difficult
ains. This
ation of all
men in the
uch help it
will not be

er elements
of the past
eated, only
y and how
remained,
and forth-
to the task
peace which
forgetting
the future
f a united

MR. BALDWIN ON THE FINISH.

Victory Of Common Sense.

STATEMENT IN PARLIAMENT.

Westminster, Wednesday.

The House of Commons was crammed this afternoon to hear the Prime Minister's announcement. The Prince of Wales sat over the clock in the Peers' Gallery and by his side was the Duke of York. Also in the Peers' Gallery was the Archbishop of Canterbury.

For a few minutes the two front benches remained half-empty while two or three items of formal business were proceeded with. Then Mr. Ramsay MacDonald, Mr. J. H. Thomas and Mr. Philip Snowden walked in to the accompaniment of a cheer from the back-bench Socialists.

A minute or two later Mr. Baldwin led a little procession of Cabinet Ministers to the Treasury Bench. As soon as the Prime Minister appeared from behind the Speaker's Chair a great shout of welcome went up from the massed Conservatives. They rose to their feet, waved order papers above their heads and cheered again and again.

That was the only bit of excitement. The statement itself and the few questions and answers that followed. it occupied only a few minutes and they were quiet and dignified. True, when Mr. Ramsay MacDonald rose to ask the Prime Minister if he had any statement to make regarding the industrial situation, Mr. Jack Jones leaped to his feet and urged his Socialist colleagues to "stand up like the other fellows did." Nobody, however, rose. Nobody wanted scenes. Parliament preserved its calm dignity as it had done from the beginning.

NATURE OF THE PEACE.

Mr Baldwin spoke so quietly that at times it was difficult to catch his words. He said :

"The President of the T.U.C. came and told me this morning that they had decided to call off the general strike forthwith. I said it would be the immediate effort of my colleagues and myself to bring about a resumption of

THE BIRTH AND LIFE OF THE "BRITISH GAZETTE"

An Unexampled Achievement In Journalism.

HOW AN IMPROVISED NEWSPAPER REACHED A CIRCULATION OF 2,209,000.

At last the moment has come to tell the story of one of the most signal exploits and adventures in the annals of English journalism—the foundation in a day and a night of a daily newspaper, *The British Gazette*, and the multiplication of its issue within a week to the stupendous total of over 2,000,000.

Nothing like it has been done before, the world over. If the exceptional occasion provided the inspiration and the opportunity, it also imposed the severest disabilities. What was done represented a triumph of resource and determination over what might well have seemed insuperable difficulties. It is a triumph of which all who had part in it have a right to be proud, and one which has served equally well two great causes.

It has defeated the attempt to keep the country in the dark during a formidable crisis in its affairs ; and it has vindicated the Press against a new conspiracy to muzzle its freedom.

Let us tell the story, which opens on Monday, May 3, under the shadow of a General Strike to be declared at midnight—a strike of which the masterstroke was to be the shutting down of the newspapers.

It was impossible to acquiesce in the prospect of a nation, exposed to the interruption of the whole of its social and industrial economy, and at the same time deprived of its news, and of the one medium through which public opinion

protection were given, to print at first 100,000 copies of a news-sheet a night, and to raise the output to 400,000 copies by the end of the week. It placed the staff of the *Morning Post* at the service of the Government, to work under its direction and authority.

THE GOVERNMENT ARRIVES.

Late that night important visitors to the Editor were announced ; and into the Editorial room marched the Chancellor of the Exchequer, Sir Samuel Hoare, Mr. J. C. C. Davidson, and a train of departmental officials. They had come to act on the suggestion of the Editor's letter ; to commandeer on behalf of His Majesty's Government the *Morning Post,* and to convert it off hand into a Government news sheet— *The British Gazette.* Sir Malcolm Fraser was put in charge as the direct representative of the Government.

The step about to be taken was a momentous one for the *Morning Post,* and hardly less so for the Government, who never before had taken responsibility for the production of a daily newspaper. In more than 150 years the *Morning Post* had but once intermitted its daily issue, and now not only were all its resources to be handed over to others, but its very name was to disappear.

Only the extreme gravity of the occasion could have justified the innovation on the one side, and the self-effacement on the other.

The act of taking over having been confirmed by a Cabinet Minute

Churchill had rejoined the Conservative party in 1923. In the general election of 1929, his whole family helped him campaign (daughter Sarah, above). But the people swept out the Conservatives, and Churchill found himself just another man in the political wilderness. He wrote at the time, "From the beginning of 1895, down to the present time of writing, I have never had time to turn around. I could almost count on my fingers the days when I have had nothing to do."

And now, he and his wife walked the quiet road.

He did more and more painting.

"Painting a picture," he said, "is like trying to fight a battle. . . . It is, if anything, more exciting. In all battles, two things are usually required of the Commander in Chief: to make a good plan for his Army and to keep a strong reserve. Both these are also obligatory upon the painter."

126

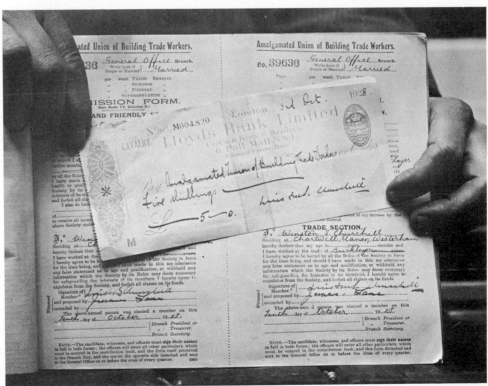

"See that wall?" he said. "You cannot imagine the amount of fun I had in building it. Apart from the actual pleasure of seeing it grow, I think I planned out a couple of books while I was laying the bricks" (with daughter Sarah). More relief for an overtired brain was to clean out the bed of an existing lake, getting his clean overalls covered with black mud, slipping on the slime, finally looking like a wet chimney sweep, but happy.

ABOVE. His home, Chartwell Manor, was commuting distance from London.   BELOW. But his study was a private world, invaded only by a secretary. One such secretary remembered that he seldom asked to have a letter read back to him after he had dictated it, that he never fumbled or asked, "What did I say?"

ABOVE. There had been five children: Randolph, Diana, Sarah, Mary (above) and Marigold. Marigold died when she was only three. At the birth of one of his daughters, Churchill met Lloyd George, who asked him, "Is she pretty?"

"Very pretty," said Churchill.

"Ah," said Lloyd George, "then she is like her mother."

"Oh, no," said Churchill, "she is like me."

Another time, he said, "All babies look like me."

BELOW. He had more time now to spend with his son (above) and daughters. His standard morning question for all of them was, "What are you doing today?" Once he found Diana (above) particularly downcast. She had nothing to do. He asked her what she would most like to do. She brightened; she wanted to go to a nightclub. He gulped, but took her and danced every dance with her until the club closed. He later learned a dance called "Underneath the Spreading Chestnut Tree," a hop-skip-and-jump dance.

ABOVE. He was upstairs in his study once, watching his wife play tennis, saw her fall, raced down the stairs so fast that he was the first to reach her, brushed everybody else aside, picked her up and carried her in.   BELOW. Later he took Clemmie on a trip to New York, and a Presidential candidate named Alfred E. Smith showed them the view from the top of the new Empire State Building.

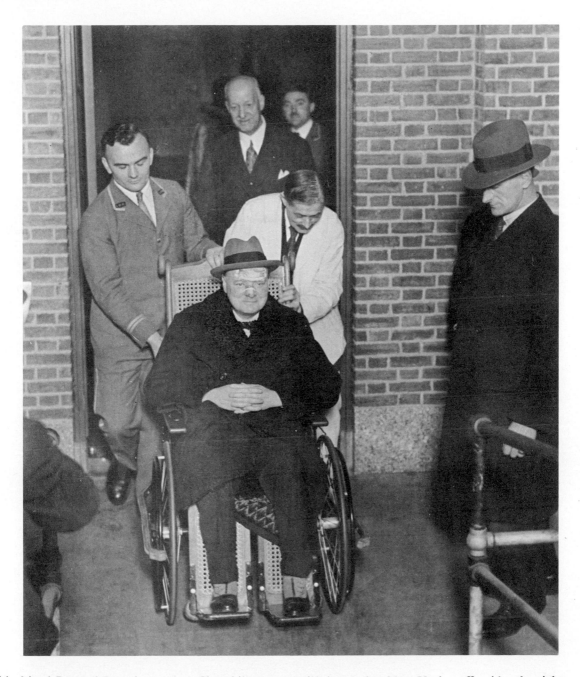

Visiting his friend Bernard Baruch one day, Churchill momentarily forgot that New York traffic rides the right side of the road (instead of the left, as in London) and was run down by a taxi on Lenox Avenue. He promptly wrote a magazine article about it, while still in the hospital.

"There was a moment of a world aglare, of a man aghast," he wrote then. "I do not understand why I was not broken like an eggshell or squashed like a gooseberry."

Dining in New York with the Duke of Windsor, many years later, Churchill heard that his valet, Norman MacGowan, was going for his first tour of the town. Churchill interrupted his dinner with the Duke to stop MacGowan in the hall and warn him, "Norman, I wanted to tell you to be careful in this New York traffic. It's very dangerous. I was knocked down here some years ago."

ABOVE. Before the Prince of Wales became king, and then Duke of Windsor, Churchill played polo with him—during this interval of more than ten years out of political office . . . BELOW. . . . hunted wild boar on the Duke of Westminster's Forest of Eu in Normandy.

The pause that refreshes . . .

ABOVE. He tiled his own roof. "I had no idea that ordinary life could be so interesting," he said.   BELOW. He had already written a two-volume biography of his father, which one critic described: "Prose still unimpaired by platform eloquence, it remains one of the best political biographies in English." Now he had time to finish a history of the First World War, *World Crisis,* and a four-volume biography of his ancestor the Duke of Marlborough, as well as the beginning of the *History of the English-Speaking People.*

Historian H. G. Wells said of Churchill's writing, "He uses words with the same daring and abandon as he does colors when he is painting. He daubs them on boldly, recklessly." Another critic called Churchill's work, ". . . historic rather than historical, glow with the making rather than the writing of history."

Of his own style, Churchill wrote, "I affected a combination of the styles of Macaulay and Gibbon, the staccato antithesis of the former and the rolling sentences and genitival endings of the latter; and I stuck in a bit of my own from time to time."

ABOVE. He had fun, too. He was driven to Ulster Hall in Belfast on an Irish jaunting car, wearing a "paddy" hat, holding a shillelagh.   BELOW. And he got all kinds of honorary degrees, this one at Oxford. He later said, "I am surprised that in my later years I should have become so good in taking degrees, because, when a schoolboy, I was so bad at passing examinations."

He went swimming at Deauville . . .

. . . and was invited everywhere to dinners and speeches. "You can't make a good speech on ice water," he once said. And, another time, "I have taken more out of alcohol than alcohol has taken out of me."

ABOVE. But his heart was elsewhere—in politics. His valet heard a rumbling from the bathtub and rushed in. "Did you want me, sir?"

Churchill looked at him. "I wasn't talking to you; I was addressing the House of Commons." BELOW. Campaigning again for his seat in the House, he found some critics still caustic about his switch back to the Conservative party: "If he changes his party with the facility of partners at a dance," wrote one critic, "he has always been true to the only party he really believes in—that which is assembled under the hat of Mr. Winston Churchill."

Another said, "It is the ultimate Churchill that escapes us. I think he escapes us for a good reason. He is not there."

But wherever he was, his wife was with him.

138

And, although they kept him out of government office, they couldn't keep him out of the House of Commons, where he sometimes actually thumbed his nose at the Opposition Members and once even stuck out his tongue.

"Yet who can say his political career is finished?" wrote one of the wiser observers. "His luck has served him so well in the past that the wheel of fortune may turn once more in his direction. He remains an uncertain quantity in British public life, a possible asset and an incalculable liability to any administration he may belong to, and a potential mutineer against any administration from which he may be excluded."

Conscious of this, the Conservative government, now back again in power, called Churchill to 10 Downing Street for occasional consultation. But they still kept him out of office—because of a disagreement he had had with them on Indian policy.

So, again, he had time to laugh with his daughter Mary .

. . . and pay his tearful respects at the funeral of his friend T. E. Lawrence of Arabia. When Churchill was Colonial Secretary, Lawrence had complimented his handling of the mess in the Middle East, of Arab claims and British interests. "In a few weeks, he made straight all the tangle," said Lawrence.

ABOVE. Now, again, he could watch his favorite goldfish . . . BELOW. . . . and paint them.

"A painting consists of two essential elements," he said. "Form and color. If you go out to paint a landscape and try to embody both, the light has changed by the time the form is looked after. So this is the idea. I go out and when I see what I want, I snap it with a camera, and at the same time make a most rapid sketch disregarding the form largely, but endeavoring to put down my impressions of the color.

"Then I have a lantern slide made of the photograph, and I darken the studio and put the slide into the lantern and then project the picture on the canvas and paint it in monotone. In this way I have the form. Then, with my color sketch before me, I put in the picture.

"I must say I like the bright colors," he added. "I rejoice with the brilliant ones and feel sorry for the poor browns.

". . . Painting is complete as a distraction. I know of nothing which, without exhausting the body, more entirely absorbs the mind."

But it couldn't absorb all his mind.

ABOVE. He was worried about the way the world was going. "Peace in her present plight must have her constables," he said. "A speedy and genuine organization of the maximum force against potential aggressors . . . offers us the sole hope of preventing war." BELOW. Working a maximum force of his own in Germany was a former Army corporal, Adolf Hitler (center, mustache) who had organized a Nazi political party strong enough to take over control of the government.

ABOVE. More and more often now, Churchill was called to consult at 10 Downing Street.   BELOW. The news was often bad . . .

LEFT. . . . and sometimes hectic.   RIGHT. But Churchill made his views pointed. "Well, I had made up my mind," said a high government official, "but then Winston came along with his hundred-horsepower brain, and what was I to do?"

OPPOSITE, BOTTOM. A Conservative M.P. said of Churchill:

"Winston hovers over our front bench like Jove among the clouds. Suddenly he drops through with a thunderclap, or a penny whistle. We never know what to expect."

Years before, when he was still a young man, he had told what people could expect of war. "Let us learn our lesson," he had written. "Never, never, never believe any war will be smooth or easy or that anyone who embarks on the strange voyage can measure the tides and hurricanes he will encounter. Once the signal is given, the statesman is no longer the master of policy but a slave of unforseeable and controllable events. Always remember, however sure you are you can easily win, that there would not be a war if the other man did not think he also had a chance."

After the British appeasement at Munich, Churchill said, "The people should know we have sustained a defeat without a war . . . they should know that we have passed an awful milestone in our history, when the whole equilibrium of Europe has been deranged, and that the terrible words have for the time been pronounced against the Western democracies: Thou are weighed in the balance and found wanting . . .

"And do not suppose that this is the end. This is only the beginning of the reckoning. This is only the first sip, the first foretaste of a bitter cup which will be proffered to us year by year unless, by a supreme recovery of moral health and martial vigor, we arise again and take our stand for freedom as in the olden time . . .

"You have been given the choice between war and dishonor. You chose dishonor and you will have war."

Churchill made his voice heard.

Not long before, in a New York newspaper interview, Churchill had said of his political limbo, "There is one thing that appeals to me strongly now, and that is I am now my own master. I am accountable to no one for what I do and the success of what I am doing depends solely upon my own efforts.

"When a man is in the Cabinet, no matter how strong he may be, he is bound to take into consideration public opinion. He may advocate measures that he firmly believes are for the public good, and he may see them work harm through the failure of someone else to carry them out properly. But the blame falls on the proposer's head, not upon the dullards who did not understand."

Daily Herald

No. 7349   •   MONDAY, SEPTEMBER 4, 1939   ONE PENNY

WAR DECLARED BY BRITAIN AND FRANCE

We Have Resolved To Finish It—PRIME MINISTER

GREAT BRITAIN DECLARED WAR ON GERMANY AT 11 O'CLOCK YESTERDAY MORNING.

Six hours later, at 5 p.m., France declared war.

Britain's resolution to defend Poland against Nazi aggression was described by the Ministry of Information in one of its first announcements, as follows :—

"At 11.15 this morning (Sunday) Mr. R. Dunbar, Head of the Treaty Department of the Foreign Office, went to the German Embassy, where he was received by Dr. Kordt, the Charge d'Affaires.

"Mr. Dunbar handed to Dr. Kordt a notification that a state of war existed between Great Britain and Germany as from 11 o'clock B.S.T. this morning. This notification constituted the formal declaration of war."

Navy Fully Mobilised

The King broadcast to the nation last night. A copy of his message, with facsimile signature, will be distributed to every household in the country.

Britain's Navy is fully mobilised and is at its war status in full strength, supplemented by a number of fully commissioned armed merchant ships as auxiliary cruisers.

The convoy system for merchant shipping has been introduced.

The Duke of Kent has taken up his war appointment.

The Empire has sprung to Britain's support. "Australia is at war," declared Mr. Menzies, the Commonwealth Prime Minister, broadcasting last night.

"Where Britain stands," he said, "there stands the people of the Empire and the British world."

"All Possible Support"

Unthinkable We Should Refuse The Challenge

—THE KING

Broadcasting last evening from his study at Buckingham Palace, the King said:—

IN this grave hour, perhaps the most fateful in our history, I send to every household of my people, both at home and overseas, this message, spoken with the same depth of feeling for each one of you as if I were able to cross your threshold and speak to you myself.

For the second time in the lives of most of us we are at war.

Over and over again we have tried to find a peaceful way out of the differences between ourselves and those who are now our enemies. But it has been in vain.

We have been forced into a conflict. For we are called with our Allies to meet the challenge of a principle which, if it were to prevail, would be fatal to any civilised order in the world.

IT is the principle which permits a State, in the selfish pursuit of power, to disregard its treaties and its solemn pledges; which sanctions the use of force or threat of force against the sovereignty and independence of other States.

Such a principle, stripped of all disguise, is surely the mere primitive doctrine that might is right; and if this principle were established throughout the world the freedom of our own country and of the whole British

WAR CABINET OF NINE

Churchill Is Now First Lord

By MAURICE WEBB
"Daily Herald" Political Correspondent

BRITAIN'S new War Cabinet, which will have full control of the conduct of hostilities, was set up yesterday.

Mr. Winston Churchill is one of the nine members. He has been appointed First Lord of the Admiralty.

Lord Hankey, who is Minister without Portfolio, is the only other member who was not in the last

POLES SMASH WAY INTO E. PRUSSIA

OFFICIALS in Warsaw stated late last night that the Polish army has smashed a way across the Northern border into East Prussia, after driving the Germans from several Polish towns in bitter fighting.

London Hears Its First Raid Warning

LONDON was calm yesterday when it heard its first air raid warning.

This is the official statement issued by the Air Ministry:—

At 11.30 a.m. yesterday an aircraft was observed approaching the South Coast.

As its identity could not be readily determined an air-raid warning was given.

It was shortly afterwards identified as a friendly aircraft and the all-clear signal was given.

BLACK-OUT TIME TO-NIGHT—7.40

BREMEN REPORTED TAKEN

THE 50,000-ton German liner Bremen is reported to have been captured by British warships.

A report to this effect was broadcast from a French wireless station last night and picked up in New York.

A "high French source" was quoted as saying that the Bremen was taken at 4 p.m., the area not being given, and was being taken to

On the Northern Front the Poles are reported to have defeated the German effort to drive a barrier across the upper part of the Corridor, by driving the Germans back across the border.

The Poles say they have broken through the German fortifications as far as the railway terminus of Deutsch Eylau.

One of the most important towns recaptured is stated to be Zbaszyn.

Dispatches from the front state that furious fighting is going on at Czestochowa and Katowice. German reports that they have captured Czestochowa are denied.

This report tells of serious air-raid casualties in Poland.

(Continued on Page 2; Earlier fighting details on Page 10)

MODERN CONCRETE CONSTRUCTION

This is an entirely new work which covers the whole field of Concrete Construction. It is essentially a practical book, and the subjects are treated from the point of view of

ENGINEERING WORKSHOP PRACTICE

This up-to-date book provides a practical source of instruction in every important branch of engineering workshop methods, materials and equipment. It deals with the

And then, one day, it came.

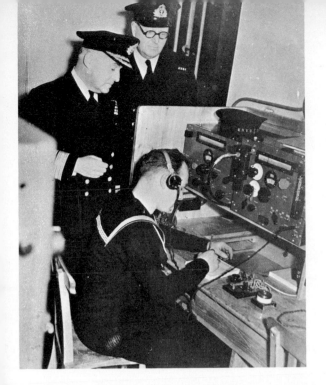

On that same day, the government decided it could no longer do without Winston Churchill and made him First Lord of the Admiralty once again. And on the telegraph sent throughout the British Navy were the words, "Winston is back . . . Winston is back. . . ."

The man Churchill called "that bloody guttersnipe" promised his people that they would rule the world for a thousand years.

On May 10, 1940, the small boy who had told his friends, "Someday I shall rule England," became Prime Minister of Great Britain.

"As I went to bed at 3 A.M.," he wrote afterwards, "I was conscious of a profound sense of relief. At last I had authority to give directions over the whole scene. I felt as if I were walking with destiny, and that all my past life had been but a preparation for this hour and for this trial. I could not be reproached either for making the war or with want of preparation for it. I thought I knew a good deal about it all, and I was sure I should not fail."

After a long stretch of phony war along the make-believe world of the Maginot line, the Nazis struck hard with tanks and France tottered and fell. Before it did, Churchill sent British troops and planes in support of General Gamelin (above). He even offered the people of France a common citizenship with England, which the government refused to consider.

Then Churchill broadcast a message:

"Frenchmen! For more than thirty years, in peace and war, I have marched with you, and I am marching still along the same road . . . We are waiting for the long-provided invasion. So are the fishes . . . Remember, we shall never stop, never weary, never give in, and that our whole people and Empire have vowed themselves to the task of cleansing Europe from the Nazi pestilence and saving the world from the new Dark Ages . . .

"Good night, then; sleep to gather strength for the morning. For the morning will come."

BELOW. To help the morning come, Churchill lent the full support of his government to a young French general who had been brought to England to coalesce the Frenchmen willing to fight for freedom, and give them hope.

153

Dunkirk: ". . . He that outlives this day and comes safe home . . .

. . . will stand a-tip-toe when this day is nam'd . . ."

"If England was what England seems . . .   . . . An' not the England of our dreams . . ."

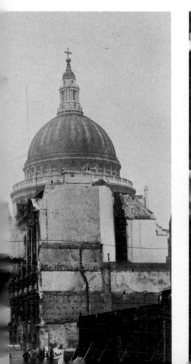

. . . This blessed plot, this earth, this realm, this England . . ."

"... 'tis true that we are in great danger ...

... the greater therefore should our courage be."

"We are fighting by ourselves alone," said Churchill to his people, "but we are not fighting *for* ourselves alone."

When a bomb destroyed the House of Commons, Churchill was moved to tears and said, "This Chamber must be rebuilt—just as it was! Meanwhile we shall not miss a single day's debate through this!"

"It was the nation and the race dwelling all round the globe that had the lion's heart," said Churchill afterwards. "I had the luck to be called upon to give the roar. I also hope I sometimes suggested to the lion the right place to use his claws."

Another English writer of a previous age had said in one of his plays, "Britain is a world by itself, and we will pay nothing for wearing our noses."

160

Shortly after he became Prime Minister, Churchill received this letter from a British soldier:

"England at last is a real nation, really led; a handful of brave, resolute men and one genuinely great man at the top. The whole rhythm of our national life has changed. We think virilely; we hold ourselves as men who know what we must face and what we must do. We are alive again. There is a meaning in poetry and sacrifice and young men going to die, and the sudden glory of a few snatched hours of leave and love."

Decorating one of these soldier-heroes, Churchill asked, "Suppose you feel pretty nervous at meeting me?"

"Yes, I do."

"Then how do you suppose I feel," said Churchill, "at meeting you?"

"We shall give it back to them . . ."

There is but one task for all—
One life for each to give.
What stands if Freedom fall?
Who dies if England live?

God of our fathers, known of old,
Lord of our far-flung battle-line,
Beneath whose awful hand we hold
Dominion over palm and pine—
Lord God of Hosts, be with us yet,
Lest we forget—lest we forget.

"I have nothing to offer but . . .

. . . blood . . .

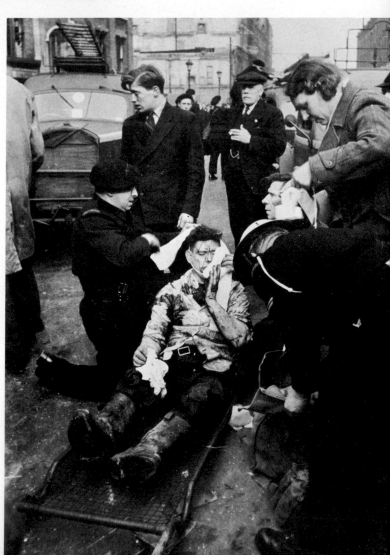

. . . toil . . .   . . . tears . . .

. . . and . . .   . . . sweat.

. . . We shall not flag or fail . . .

. . . We shall fight on the seas and oceans . . .

. . . We shall fight with growing confidence and growing strength in the air . . .

. . . We shall defend our island whatever the cost may be . . .

. . . We shall fight on the landing grounds . . .

. . . We shall fight on the beaches . . .

. . . We shall fight in the fields . . .

. . . and in the streets . . .

. . . We shall fight in the hills . . .

. . . We shall never surrender.

Let us therefore brace ourselves to our duties, and so bear ourselves that if the British Empire and its Commonwealth last for a thousand years, men will say . . .

. . . This was their finest hour."

Dear Churchill,

Wendell Willkie will give you this. . . . I think this verse applies t
your people as it does to us:

"Sail on, O ship of State!
Sail on, O union strong and great!
Humanity with all its fears,
With all the hopes of future years,
Is hanging breathless on thy fate!"

As ever yours,

FRANKLIN D. ROOSEVELT

Churchill and Franklin D. Roosevelt met aboard ship "somewhere in the Atlantic" to frame an Atlantic Charter of principles of freedom. Their Sunday prayer: "God our strength in ages past . . ."

Peace on earth to men of good will.

WITH THE BEST OF GOOD WISHES

FOR

CHRISTMAS AND THE NEW YEAR

from

Winston Churchill

"ATLANTIC MEETING"

When she had accepted Winston Churchill's proposal of marriage so many years before, she had told him, "Now I have got you. The trouble will be to keep you." To which he replied, "You will find that no trouble, my dear."

What trouble there was, they shared.

His youngest daughter, Mary, rated a Prime Minister's salute . . .

. . . and a father's embrace.

His other daughter saw service too (Sarah, below).

And his son, Randolph, was a British commando officer in the Middle East.

Touring the Middle East, Churchill told the Tommies there, "After the war, when a man is asked what he did, it will be quite sufficient for him to say, "I marched and fought with the Desert Army." He gave them one of the two Churchill gestures that were to become international symbols of hope: the hat waving on his cane . . .

. . . and, to some sailors, his V sign for Victory.

ABOVE. He went back to the United States to see his new friend. Mrs. Roosevelt said of the two of them: "Nobody around them would dare to say, 'I'm afraid.' " F.D.R. later said he caught up on his work while Churchill napped, and he caught up on his sleep after Churchill left. BELOW. They became fast friends. They both loved the Navy, history, the outdoors, nonsense rhymes. Long before, when Churchill was First Lord of the Admiralty, F.D.R. had written him, "It is because you and I occupied similar positions in the World War that I want you to know how glad I am that you are back again in the Admiralty." And, in his postscript, F.D.R. added, "I am glad you did the Marlborough volumes before this thing started—and I much enjoyed reading them."

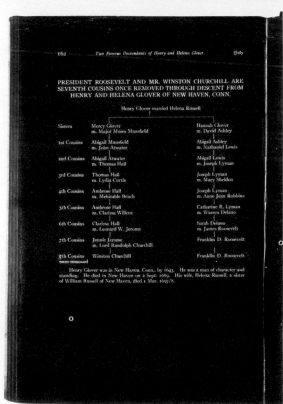

**PRESIDENT ROOSEVELT AND MR. WINSTON CHURCHILL ARE
SEVENTH COUSINS ONCE REMOVED THROUGH DESCENT FROM
HENRY AND HELENA GLOVER OF NEW HAVEN, CONN.**

Henry Glover married Helena Russell

Sisters	Mercy Glover m. Major Moses Mansfield	Hannah Glover m. David Ashley
1st Cousins	Abigail Mansfield m. John Atwater	Abigail Ashley m. Nathaniel Lewis
2nd Cousins	Abigail Atwater m. Thomas Hall	Abigail Lewis m. Joseph Lyman
3rd Cousins	Thomas Hall m. Lydia Curtis	Joseph Lyman m. Mary Sheldon
4th Cousins	Ambrose Hall m. Mehitable Beach	Joseph Lyman m. Anne Jean Robbins
5th Cousins	Ambrose Hall m. Clarissa Willcox	Catharine R. Lyman m. Warren Delano
6th Cousins	Clarissa Hall m. Leonard W. Jerome	Sarah Delano m. James Roosevelt
7th Cousins	Jennie Jerome m. Lord Randolph Churchill	Franklin D. Roosevelt
7th Cousins once removed	Winston Churchill	Franklin D. Roosevelt

Henry Glover was in New Haven, Conn., by 1643. He was a man of character and
standing. He died in New Haven on 2 Sept. 1689. His wife, Helena Russell, a sister
of William Russell of New Haven, died 1 Mar. 1697/8.

ABOVE. At one dinner elsewhere, Churchill looked at a lovely salmon and said, "That is indeed a magnificent fish.
I must have some of him. No! No! I will have meat. Carnivores will win this war."

At another time, Churchill walked into the White House bathroom nude, to find F.D.R. already there, and
reportedly said, "The Prime Minister of Great Britain has nothing to hide from the President of the United States."
BELOW. Besides, they were seventh cousins.

Churchill addressed the joint session of the United States Congress seventeen days after the Japanese had attacked Pearl Harbor. "It was with heart stirrings that I fulfilled the invitation to address the Congress of the United States," he told them. "I have never addressed a foreign parliament before. Yet, to me, who could trace unbroken male descent on my mother's side through five generations, from a lieutenant who served in George Washington's Army, it was possible to feel a blood-right to speak to the representatives of the great republic in our common cause." And he added later: "I wish indeed that my mother, whose memory I cherish across the veil of years, could have been here to see me."

White House staffers still remember Winston Churchill on the lawn, dancing a jig in his siren suit when the war news was good.

"I wore a suit like this to the Kremlin once," he said. "It didn't go so well. They thought I was pushing democracy too far."

Robert Gordon Menzies, who was to be Prime Minister of Australia, remembered another incident:

"I will never forget how, clad in his famous and almost comic-opera 'siren suit,' he would enter the historic Cabinet room at Downing Street, take his seat in dead silence, pull his truculent and tilted cigar from his mouth, turn his light bright-blue eyes around the table and say, 'Gentlemen, we have the signal honor of being responsible for our country at a time of deadly danger, and of bad news. We will proceed with the business.' "

Another time, in firing a Cabinet minister, he told him, "I did not suffer from any desire to be relieved of my responsibilities. All I wanted was compliance with my wishes after reasonable discussion."

He inspected the newly arrived American troops under the command of a young general, Dwight D. Eisenhower . . .

. . . and inspected his own British commandos, en route to hit-and-run raids on the coast of France:

> Once more into the breach, dear friends, once more;
> Or close the wall up with our English dead.
> . . . Imitate the action of the tiger:
> Stiffen the sinews, summon up the blood.

10, Downing Street,
Whitehall.

February 23, 1944.

My dear Franklin,

  Clemmie suggested to me that we should send you
this photograph of some of the rooms of 10, Downing Street
after the bombs fell last Sunday night, as it contains a
copy of the picture of us both at Argentia.   The carpet in
the foreground is the one given me by the Shah at Teheran;
luckily it is undamaged.

  It is surprising what curious blast effects have
followed from these few bombs.   Places as much as 500 yards
away have been affected, while others quite close to have
been missed out.   They were very quick at clearing up all
the mess and we are back again.

    Yours always

    W.

The President of the United States of America.

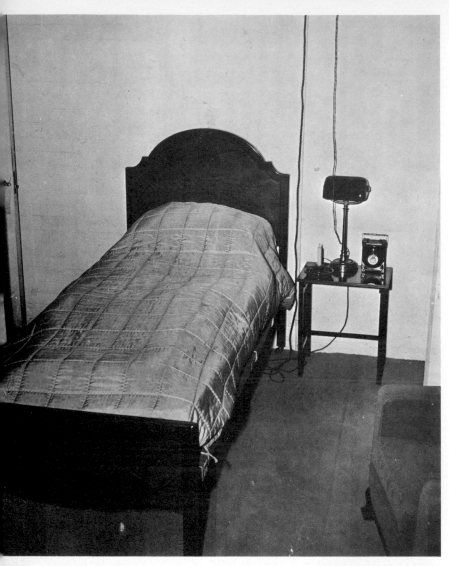

Air-raid shelter: His and . . .

. . . Hers

ABOVE. The D-day discussions for the invasion of France, discussed long before in the United States with General George Marshall (left) and Secretary of War Stimson (with pith helmet) . . . BELOW. . . . now intensified into detail.

ABOVE. "Fair stood the wind for France . . ."   BELOW. And then they were ready.

"... I would give all my fame ...
... for a pot of ale and safety ..."

V for Victory: "Victory at all costs, Victory in spite of all terror, Victory however long the road may be; for without Victory there is no survival."

H hour, D day:

ABOVE. And he had to see it for himself.   BELOW. "O God of battles! Steel my soldiers' hearts; possess them not with fear."

ABOVE. In France, he had friends.   BELOW. At the Siegfried line: "The proud German Army, by its sudden collapse, sudden crumbling and breaking up, has once again proved the truth of the saying, 'The Hun is either at your throat or at your feet.' "

ABOVE. With glee, he wrote: "A present for Hitler—Churchill." BELOW. Eisenhower refused to let him cross the Rhine, because of the heavy shellfire. Churchill simply waited until Eisenhower left, then crossed with Field Marshal Montgomery (beret). A German shell landed fifty yards away, but somebody reported, "Churchill seemed more perturbed about lighting his cigar in the wind than he was about the shellfire."

"The last time I was on the Rhine," Churchill told the American soldiers, "was at Cologne during the last war. We cruised fifty miles upstream in a British gunboat."

In World War I, Churchill had promoted an unsuccessful invasion through Europe's "soft under-belly"; now, again, he tried to promote a similar invasion in that area, and was vetoed. But he still kept a close eye on the area, met with Greek government leaders in an unheated, unlit room in Athens in December, 1944, to help them in their fight against Communist-oriented rebels.

He asked his diplomatic aide, "This Greek leader, this Archbishop, is he a simple man of God, or is he one of those crafty, scheming, political prelates?"

"I'm afraid," said his aide, "that His Grace is one of the latter."

"Good," said Churchill. "Then he's just our man."

ABOVE. He went to Moscow, too, to see Marshal Stalin. Afterwards, Churchill wired Eisenhower: "I deem it highly important that we should shake hands with the Russians as far east as possible." BELOW. Back in France, the mood was warmer, the memories deeper. The young General de Gaulle had grown into a leader of greatness.

ABOVE. At the Yalta Conference, with the war's end near, Churchill was buoyant . . . BELOW. . . . but his great American friend seemed drawn, almost ill. . . .

Then, on Friday the 13th, April, 1945, the phone rang at 3 A.M. in the room of Churchill's bodyguard, Inspector Walter Thompson. Churchill wanted him to come quickly. Thompson grabbed his guns and rushed in, to find Churchill silently pacing the room back and forth, back and forth, his head sunk.

"Have you heard the terrible news, Thompson?" he said, his eyes wet, staring at the rug. "It's the President of the United States. Your friend and mine, Thompson. He has passed away." And then he added slowly, "He died on the eve of victory, but he saw the wings of it. And he heard them."

Teheran.

1 December, 1943

My dear Franklin,

    I was indeed touched by your kind present. It is a beautiful bowl, and I shall always treasure it as a reminder of our sunlit days in Teheran and of the most memorable of my Birthdays

    I cannot thank you enough for all your friendship and support in the years in which we have worked together, and I am glad of this occasion to send you a message of sincere affection and gratitude.

Yours always

Winston S. Churchill

The President of the United States of America.

"Long live the cause of freedom. God save the King."

Churchill later told a crowd of fifty thousand in Whitehall: "This is your victory, victory in the cause of freedom in every land. In all our long history, we have never seen a greater day than this. Everyone has done their bit. Everyone has tried. Neither the long years, nor the dangers, nor the fierce attacks of the enemy have in any way weakened the resolve of the British nation. God bless you all."

ABOVE. There were still the postwar problems to discuss at Potsdam with a new President of the United States, Harry S. Truman, and the same Stalin. Early in the war, Stalin had told Churchill: "You know, Mr. Churchill, you've said many unkind things about me in your time."

"Ah, yes, quite true," said Churchill, "but you weren't on our side then." BELOW. For Churchill (lower left), there was still the question of whose side Stalin was now on. Long before, in 1939, he had described Soviet Russia as "... a riddle wrapped in a mystery inside an enigma."

Eight days after Potsdam, July, 1945, the British held a general election. "When I was called upon to be Prime Minister," Churchill had said, "there were not many applicants for the job. Since then perhaps the market has improved."

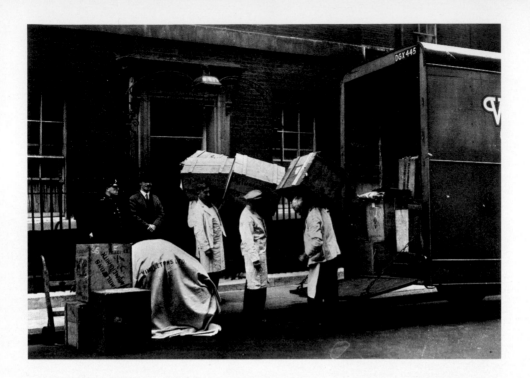

The British people, surprisingly, voted Churchill and his Conservative party out of office. Masking his bitterness, Churchill said, "I regret that I have not been permitted to finish the work against Japan."

To his Cabinet, he said, "This is our Dunkirk."

To a friend, he said, "Although always prepared for martyrdom, I preferred that it should be postponed."

And when King George VI offered him a Knight of the Garter, he said, "I can hardly accept the Garter from the King after the people have given me the boot."

He was now many times a grandfather . . .

. . . and now even his little Mary had a baby to christen.

ABOVE. Despite his fabulous wardrobe of clothes and uniforms, he usually preferred his zipper suit and a favorite hat that was more than thirty years old—but he did go for embroidered slippers. He still superstitiously tapped wood, still loved his real turtle soup, still had breakfast alone. "My wife and I tried two or three times to have breakfast together," he said, "but we had to stop or our marriage would have been wrecked." BELOW. And he could still make a campaign speech—this time for his son, Randolph (seated on the stage with his son Winston).

One critic said of his painting, "There's no depth to it—it's all slap." But Churchill said of his paints and brushes, "These are my toys. I believe that as long as a man can play with toys, that long will he remain young."

He had also said, "Human beings may be divided into three classes—those who are toiled to death, those who are worried to death and those who are bored to death. Happy are the painters, for they shall not be lonely."

And, still another time, he wrote, "When I get to Heaven, I mean to spend a considerable portion of my first million years in painting and so get to the bottom of the subject."

221

To J.D.R.

from WSC.

"A fresh egg from the faithful hen!"

Quebec 1944

ABOVE. His own books, which filled much of these shelves, earned for him a Nobel Prize in Literature, describing him as ". . . a modern Caesar who also has the gift of wielding Cicero's stylus."

Churchill answered, "I am proud, but also, I admit, awe-struck at your decision to include me. I do hope you are right. I feel we are both running a considerable risk and that I do not deserve it. But I shall have no misgivings, if you have none."

To young writers, Churchill also had some advice: "Broadly speaking, the short words are best and the old words are best of all."

To prize-givers everywhere, he added, "Give the prizes to the men who make you proudest of being a member of the human race." BELOW. In the Franklin D. Roosevelt Library in Hyde Park, there is a book by Churchill with the above inscription.

222

ABOVE. The former subaltern of the 21st Lancers who rode in one of the last great cavalry charges at Omdurman proved that he still could ride a horse. BELOW. He also bought them and raced them. His first horse, Colonist II, was a champion colt at Ascot. When Colonist lost the next year's Ascot, Churchill, as an excuse, said that he had had a serious talk with the horse just before the race. "I told him: 'This is a very big race and, if you win it, you will never have to run again. You will spend the rest of your life in agreeable female company.' " Then Churchill added wryly, "Colonist II did not keep his mind on the race."

ABOVE. At a party, Churchill asked if they had enough beer, and they said Yes. Churchill shook his head and said, "Nonsense, there is never enough beer. Get some more." BELOW. And he could still appreciate some of the other pleasurable things in life.

ABOVE. He still had a good aim in the traditional British dart game. BELOW. And when a photographer said, "I hope to take your picture on your hundredth birthday," Churchill answered, "I see no reason why you shouldn't, young man—you look hale and hearty enough."

But still, there was a restlessness, a loneliness.

"It is never possible for a man to recover his lost position," he had written of his father.

But what was true of his father turned out not to be true of him.

ABOVE. "It's no use doing what you like," he had once said. "You have to like what you do." He liked politics. In Britain's general election in 1951, he campaigned with vigor. To the people, he said, "I do not believe that we are at the end of all our glories. BELOW. The people remembered, and the emotion was mutual.

And so, again, Winston Leonard Spencer Churchill was Prime Minister of Great Britain. He had a quip ready. He remembered a story of a British officer in the Balkans, talking to a lady after the previous election, when he had been thrown out, and the lady had said, "Poor Mr. Churchill, I suppose now he will be shot." Churchill added, "My friend was able to reassure her by saying that the sentence might be mitigated by various forms of hard labor."

"At all times," he had elsewhere said, "according to my lights and throughout the changing scenes through which we are all hurried, I have always faithfully served two public causes, which, I think, stand supreme—the maintenance of the enduring greatness of Britain and her Empire, and the historical continuity of our Island life."

ABOVE. In the United States, he refused to make any comment on the upcoming national election. Of a previous election, he had said, "I am not going to choose between Republicans and Democrats—I want the lot." He visited President Truman aboard the yacht Williamsburg, where they posed in front of a picture of a sea battle between British and American ships in the War of 1812. Of Anglo-American unity now, he had said, "If we are together, nothing is impossible, and if we are divided, all will fail." BELOW. At the New York home of his oldest American friend, Bernard Baruch, he had a reunion with his former Army friend, the newly elected President of the United States, Dwight D. Eisenhower.

Later, he and his old friend looked out of the window at the passing parade. A reporter had asked seventy-six-year-old Churchill whether he had any plan for retirement. "Not until I am a great deal worse," said Churchill, "and the Empire, a great deal better."

Asked by another reporter whether he had any fear of death, Churchill answered, "I am ready to meet my Maker. Whether my Maker is prepared for the great ordeal of meeting me is another matter."

Back home in England, his wife was waiting for him at the dock in Southampton. Speaking at her old school on living with greatness, Lady Churchill had said, "If you find yourself in conflict with men, never become aggressive in your rivalry. She who forces her point may well lose her advantage."

There was still a cold war to fight, a European alliance to strengthen, the heads of state to see. He traveled constantly, and everywhere.

When people asked how he managed it at his age, he said:

"You must hire a deputy and make him be at your desk at eight. He acts for you while you stay in bed and work from there. Have a secretary come to your home and bring the mail and be in touch with your office by telephone. Let it be known that your office-arrival time is eleven thirty.

"You must sleep some time between lunch and dinner—and no halfway measure. Take off your clothes and get into bed. Don't think you will be doing less work; you will be able to do more. You will get two days in one, or at least one and a half.

"When the war started, I had to sleep during the day out of necessity—so that I could work far into the night. But a man should sleep during the day also to be at his best in the evening, when he joins his wife and friends at dinner. A good meal, with good wines, then some brandy—that is the great moment of the day."

ABOVE. Somebody once asked him how many cigars he smoked and he said, "Fourteen, and I like every one of them." He later modified that, saying, "The number of cigars I smoke is wholly dependent upon the length and size—and certain other conditions." Actually, he smoked them halfway. He said his father had once wanted to give up smoking, but that, if he had, "I might have been bad-tempered at the wrong time."

A headline in *The New York Times* during this period read:

CHURCHILL SUFFERING
FROM PNEUMONIA:
SMOKES TWO CIGARS

BELOW. "You have the songs," he told the students in his annual trip to Harrow. "They are wonderful, marvelous, more than could be put into bricks and mortar, or treasured in any trophies of silver or gold. They grow with the years. I treasure them and sing them with joy."

The boys at Harrow added a new verse to one of their songs, dedicated to Churchill, part of which read:

> Younger at heart, you return to the hill;
> You who, in days of defeat, ever bolder,
> Led us to victory, serve Britain still.

He was Mr. England and they wanted to pat his back . . .

. . . touch his hand.

But the time had come . . .

. . . and he left 10 Downing Street for the last time as Prime Minister.

"In war, Resolution. In defeat, Defiance. In victory, Magnanimity. In peace, Good Will."

"I'm glad you have your medals on," he told the ex-serviceman. "I always wear mine."

A favorite of his paintings: the tapestry at Blenheim Palace.

They celebrated their golden wedding anniversary in 1958. One of the mistaken judgments of their time was the comment of a critic at their wedding, who said of them, "There are two lively chips. The marriage will not last a month."

"I made the two most important decisions of my life at Blenheim," he said. "One was to be born there, and the other, to marry. I have never had cause to regret either."

"I have pursued life, not without pleasure . . ."

. . . and not without greatness.

From Queen Victoria . . .

. . . to Queen Elizabeth, he had served six sovereigns.

And now he belongs to history.